FINISHES in the ETHNIC TRADITION

by
**Suzanne Baizerman
and Karen Searle**

Braid with stitched tassels, an embellishment from a
Bolivian coca bag.

Cover Photo: Buttonhole stitch variation used as a
decorative join on a Guatemalan skirt.

Illustrations by Suzanne Baizerman
Photographs by Karen Searle

Acknowledgements

In the early '70s, Bucky King and Susan Gilmurray taught a one-day workshop at the Weavers Guild of Pittsburgh entitled "Finishes and Embellishments." The seeds for this book were planted in that workshop and in their subsequent article for *Shuttle, Spindle and Dyepot*. We are grateful to them for focusing our attention on finishes as an entity, and for forever sensitizing us to the finishes that weavers use.

In the ensuing years, we became acquainted with additional finishes in all kinds of fiber literature. Through our museum work with textiles from all over the world, additional examples of finishing were uncovered. We developed a course in finishing techniques at the Weavers Guild of Minnesota. Since then, our generous students have been a constant source of new material for finishes and their applications.

We are grateful to everyone who loaned us textiles to study and photograph, and particularly to the Science Museum of Minnesota and to Vesterheim, the Norwegian-American Museum in Decorah, Iowa.

We are also grateful to all of those who helped us in the preparation of this book; especially to Dianne Swanson, Margaret Pidde, and our patient husbands for assistance beyond the call of duty.

Turkish Nomads' camel harness, card woven. Decorated with pom-poms. *Courtesy of Charlotte Jirousek.*

Contents

Plates   (pages 25-28)

Plate 1: Donkey Saddle Blanket, Turkey, with warp protectors of Alternated Overhand Knots, ending with Plied Warp Ends. *Courtesy of Charlotte Jirousek.*

Plate 2: Ancient Stitch joins the two sections of a contemporary Peruvian *manta* in warp-faced weave wool. *Authors' collection.*

Plate 3: A Philippine Edge is used as a weft protector as well as an embellishment in this Mexican tortilla cloth made of fine cotton in a warp-faced weave. *Authors' collection.*

Plate 4: Bolivian coca bag has yarn embellishments stitched onto the bottom, with long strands wrapped in many color s for additional embellishment. *Authors' collection.*
Plate 4a: Detail,Wrapped embellishment on Bolivian coca bag.

Plate 5: A weft-faced band with weft loops for fringe is an interesting addition to this pre-Colombian open-weave fragment. *Courtesy of the Science Museum of Minnesota, St. Paul, Minnesota.*

Plate 6: Monkey's Fist buttons used in "frog" closings from Chinese garments. *Courtesy of Suzy Sewell.*

Plate 7: Guided Half Hitch used to form a lacy border on this wool shawl from Mexico. *Courtesy of Helen van den Berg.*

Plate 8: An Israeli saddle bag in a weft-faced weave features Buttonhole Stitch edgings and joins, and Wrapped Tassels. *Authors' collection.*

Plate 9: Tiny woven bands with weft-loop fringes athe adorn a Chinese medallion, itself an embellishment for a garment. *Courtesy of Margaret McCutchan.*

Plate 10: Detail, seam of a Guatemalan *huipil*, or woman's blouse, joined with Figure-Eight Stitch. *Authors' collection.*

Plate 11: A Buttonhole stitch variation in silk forms a colorful seam decoration on Guatemalan skirt. *Courtesy of the Science Museum of Minnesota, St. Paul, Minnesota.*

Plate 12: Alternated Overhand Knots form a geometric pattern at the border of a finely-woven cotton shawl from Mexico. *Courtsey of Helen van den Berg.*

Plate 13: Detail of a closure on a Chinese garment. Monkey's Fist buttons and loops are made from the garment fabric, and are wrapped; with colored thread for decoration. The edges are turned up on the right side and secured with a decorative Buttonhole Stitch variation. *Courtesy of Margaret McCutchan.*

Plate 14: *Firfletting*, or fringe braiding, is a series of Four-Strand flat braids joined, separated and rejoined, used as a warp protector on an 18th or 19th-Century textile from Norway, woven of coarse linen. *Courtesy of Vesterheim, the Norwegian-American Museum, Decorah, Iowa.*

Plate 15: The Damascus Edge is used as a finish on a contemporary Swedish tapestry. The warp ends were woven back into the cloth after a row of knots was made. *Courtsey of Lindy Westgard.*

Plate 16: Augmented Overhand Knots add color to this fine cotton textile from Cyprus. *Courtesy of Nancy Symeonides.*

Plate 17: Small tufts of yarn have been sewn into the bottom of a contemporary Peruvian coca bag, and stitched to form tassels. *Authors' collection.*

Plate 18: Kashugi bag, 19th Century Turkey, woven in Soumak and Pile, embellished with Eight-Strand braids ending in stitched tassels. *Courtesy of Charlotte Jirousek.*

Plate 19: Detail of the yoke of a Mexican blouse. Sections are joined together with the Buttonhole Stitch. The edges are hemmed in an overcasting variation. *Authors' collection.*

Plate 20: Plied fringe on a Norwegian headscarf, ca. 1885. *Courtesy of Vesterheim, the Norwegian-American Museum, Decorah, Iowa.*

Plate 21: A Rolled Hem n a contrasting color , and decorated with embroidery, trims anotherwise plain Chinese textile. *Courtesy of Margaret McCutchan.*

Plate 22: Guatemalan Tassels in various warp colors are added to make a lively border on a cotton shawl from Guatemala. *Courtesy of Shari Kohnen.*

Plate 23: Ghanaian Kente Cloth is made of strips of finely-woven weft-faced and balanced weave cotton cloth joined inconspicuously with an Overcastring Stitch. *Courtesy of Pam Prosser-Shonoiki.*

Plate 24: Twining is used as a weft protector and a warp spacer in this Navajo blanket. *Courtesy of Lindy Westgard.*

Plate 25: A Tubular Band edging, right, and a Flat Band edging, left, both in crossed-warp weaves, are woven onto the four selvage edges of two Bolivian *mantas. Collection of Adele Cahlander. Photo by Adele Cahlander.*

Plate 26: Bolivian coca bag joined at the sides with VanDyke Stitch. The top is edged with a Tubular Band. Bolivian pom-poms and Wrapping complete the embellishment. *Authors' collection.*
Plate 26a: Detail of Bolivian pom-pom embellishment.

Plate 27: Detail of a 19th-Century apron from Turkey, its two panels joined by the Ancient Stitch. Augmented Overhand Knots fill out the bottom fringe. *Courtesy of Charlotte Jirousek.*

Plate 28: A woven fringe with unusually shaped tabs is added to thie pre-Colombian Peruvian tapestry fragment. *Courtesy of the Science Museum of Minnesota, St. Paul, Minnesota.*

Plate 29: Feather Stitch used to decorate the seams of a Mexican shirt. *Courtesy of Eileen Flory.*

Plate 30: Buttonhole Stitches and Herringbone Stitches decorate and join seams of felt mittens by Northwest Coast Eskimos, Ft. Simpson, Canada. *Courtesy of Katie Knopke.*

Plate 31: Crocheted joins enhance the seams of a wool felt Greek jacket *Courtesy of Katherine Simon Frank.*

Plate 32: A pre-Colombian fragment adorned with woven fringe, or tabs. *Courtesy of the Science Museum of Minnesota, St. Paul, Minnesota.*

Introduction

High in the Bolivian altiplano a weaver removes a four selvage piece from the loom. It is destined to be a *chuspa* or coca bag. But the act of taking the weaving from the loom is not an act of completion. Rather, it is the beginning of a further creative process, the finishing process. Perhaps she will weave a tubular edge and a strap; there might be tassels to form. This weaver learned as a child not only the way to weave but the way to finish the piece; this is the way to make a *chuspa*. When all of this careful finishing work is completed the piece is ready to assume its cultural role--perhaps as a gift to the weaver's bethrothed.

Too often weavers caught up in our highly technological society want quick results. Emphasis may fall on dexterity with the loom rather than on integration of a woven piece as a whole. In our culture we are often expected to be more individualistic, more self-expressive in our work. In contrast the Bolivian weaver knows from cultural tradition what her piece will look like from start to finish before she begins. And cultural norms and values monitor her standards of craftsmanship.

We have entitled this book *Finishes in the Ethnic Tradition* because we hope to establish the same kind of high standards for completing hand woven goods as those that are used in the fine ethnic textiles we have studied in museums, in our travels and in private collections. Our goal is to broaden your repertoire of finishes by looking to other cultures, present and past, for ideas and inspiration. We will present a variety of techniques--some ornate, some inconspicuous. We hope that from the initial conception of your work you will then have finishing techniques in mind and produce a beautifully integrated piece--*In the Ethnic Tradition*.

1

By finishing, we mean any manipulation or addition applied to a woven piece once it is taken from the loom. There may be a lot or a little finishing added to a piece, but whatever we do, it should suit the needs of the piece. Finishing should be a means of emphasizing the materials used in a piece, enlivening the piece, introducing a new material or color, or camouflaging (seams, that is, not poor craftsmanship!). Some of our work has a need for elaborate finishes, and some for subtle finishes. We need to have both at our fingertips.

This book is divided into four main parts.
PART I deals with finishes done on the loom and weft protectors. Weft protectors are operations that we do to hold the weft in place. Often this is a preparation for fringe or hems.
PART II is concerned with warp protectors. This most often means fringe treatments of one sort or another.
PART III presents some joins for seaming our pieces of fiberwork together
PART IV presents some yarn embellishments that may be added to our projects. Some are fanciful and some are more practical.
The *INDEX* is cross-referenced for ease in locating the techniques.
An *APPENDIX* on making a sampler of finishing techniques to accompany this book has been included in the hope that such an addition will enhance the reference value of this work.

Each illustration in this book indicates the type of fabric on which the finishing technique is usually found, i.e. warp faced, weft faced or balanced weave fabric.

It is often necessary to think about the finishing of a piece before the weaving is begun. Allowances for fringes, joins or hems must be planned, and, the finishes should integrate with the rest of the piece. The warp and/or weft yarns or materials that complement them are best for most finishing purposes.

While the project is on the loom, we also think about finishes. For example, selvages may be an important part of the piece. This may mean concentrating on even, plain selvages, or it may mean working for more ornate scalloped edges. *A decorative scalloped edge can be made by weaving with three shuttles*, as shown in figure 1.

Note: When working with the warp and weft protectors in the pages that follow, it is wise to weight the piece being working on with a brick, some books or even a sand bag or bag of shot. The warp ends of the piece should hang down from the edge of the work table.

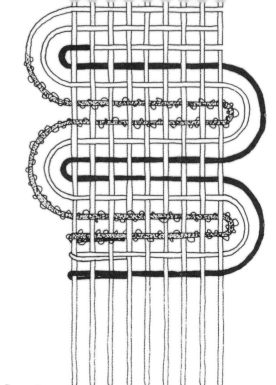

Figure 1

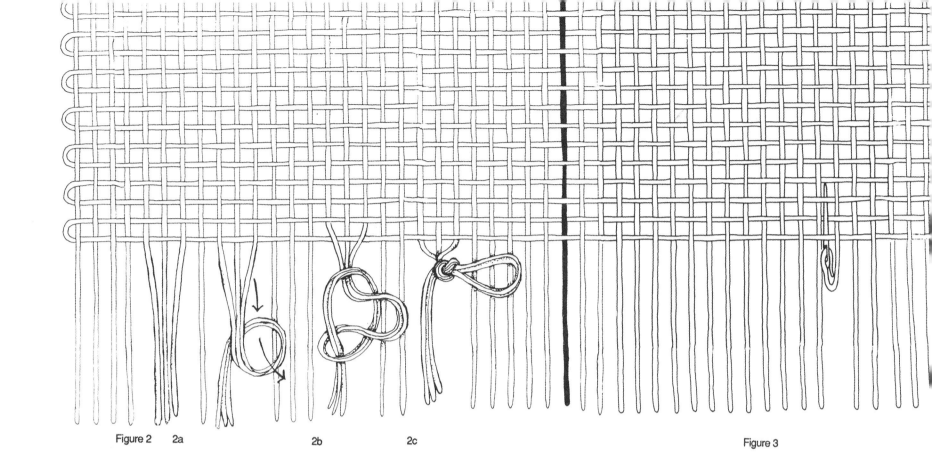

Figure 2   2a   2b   2c   Figure 3

PART I:
Weft Protectors

Weft protectors are used when the basic concern is to keep the weft from unravelling in a woven piece.

TEMPORARY WEFT PROTECTORS
Measures that are used to hold the weft in place until the final finishing can be done are called temporary weft protectors. These may be *slip knots*, as shown in figure 2a-d, or a bit of *glue* applied along the fell lines of the piece. Beginning and ending a weaving with some *rag strips or heavy yarn* that will later be removed will also serve as a temporary weft protector.

PERMANENT WEFT PROTECTORS
Permanent weft protectors can be divided into the following categories: *Handstitched, Knotted, Bound, Woven, Sewn*. Many provide a decorative edging while also holding the weft in place.

As a foundation for permanent weft protectors, the first and last rows of a piece can be beaten more firmly. The weft protectors used can be the final step in the finishing process, or they may serve as a foundation for further finishes such as fringe or braids.

The permanent weft protectors *allow for weaving the warp ends back into the cloth*. See figure 3. This in itself is a good way to protect the weft. For a fabric of very fine yarns, weaving one warp end back into the cloth every inch or so will provide a very inconspicuous finish.

Handstitched Weft Protectors

A long strand of weft yarn or a matching sewing thread may be used for the handstitched protectors. The stitching is easier to do on the loom while the work is still under tension. If, like many weavers, you have trouble disciplining yourself to stop weaving and stitch, use a temporary weft protector at each end of the piece and stitch after the piece is off the loom.

To handstitch on the loom:
Leave an end of weft at least four times the width of the piece at the right side when you begin. Weave one or two inches. Stop and work the handstitched weft protector at the end of the cloth nearest you. Then proceed to weave your entire piece. Before removing it from the loom, stitch at the other end.

Please note that the illustrations in this section are intended only as a guide. The number of warp ends and weft rows covered by the stitches can be varied to suit the scale of the fabric being worked on.

Note: In each illustration on this page, stitching proceeds from right to left.

SEWN WARP ENDS
One way to protect the weft with handstitching is to *sew through each warp end* (fig. 4).

BUTTONHOLE STITCH
The familiar Buttonhole or Blanket Stitch is an excellent weft protector (fig. 5). *The stitches are worked from the bottom up.* An attractive edging is created with this stitch. Plate 13 shows this edging and its variations used in a finely woven textile from China. Plate 8 shows a buttonhole edging on a heavy, weft faced bag from Israel; Plate 30 shows it used on felted Eskimo mittens.

OVERCASTING
The Overcast Stitch is the quickest of the handstitched protectors (fig. 6). *The stitches are made from the top of the fabric down.* By reversing the direction of the stitching, a crosstitch effect will result.

Figure 4   Figure 5   Figure 6

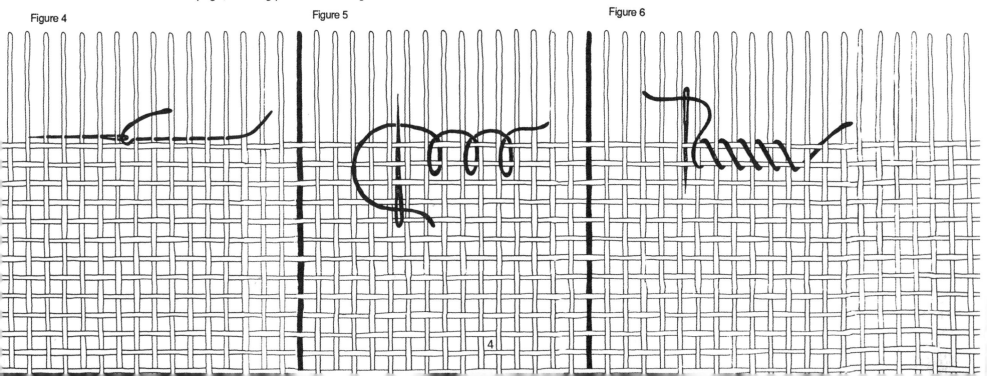

HEMSTITCHING

A Hemstitched edge is the most secure of the handstitched protectors, and easily the most popular one. Take the time to master it.

It is a two-step process: *the stitching thread sews into the weft, then it encircles the warp* (fig. 7). It may not seem right at first, but each successive stitch will tighten the previous one. Use a heavy yarn to hemstitch for a raised, embroidered effect; use sewing thread for an invisible secure edge.

The illustration below shows one of many variations on the hemstitch. Others may be found in the De Dillmont book listed in the bibliography, which shows hemstitching used in its traditional form as a fabric decoration.

Knotted Weft Protectors

Tying knots in the warp ends of a piece is one of the most natural and frequently used ways of protecting the weft. Many interesting knotting techniques were used in the pieces that we examined. Peter Collingwood includes a lot of information on knotted weft protectors in his rug weaving book listed in the bibliography.

A rhythm develops as you do the knotted weft protectors, so stick with it--you will come to enjoy them!

Knotted weft protectors are used primarily on rugs. However, they can also be used for other weft-faced weave projects such as handbags, pilllows, tapestries, etc. They form a ridge at the edge of the weaving and are a good base for fringe if it is to be applied later on. A few knotted protectors are good for warp-faced fabrics.

Note: In this example the hemstitching proceeds from right to left.   Figure 7: 7b   7a

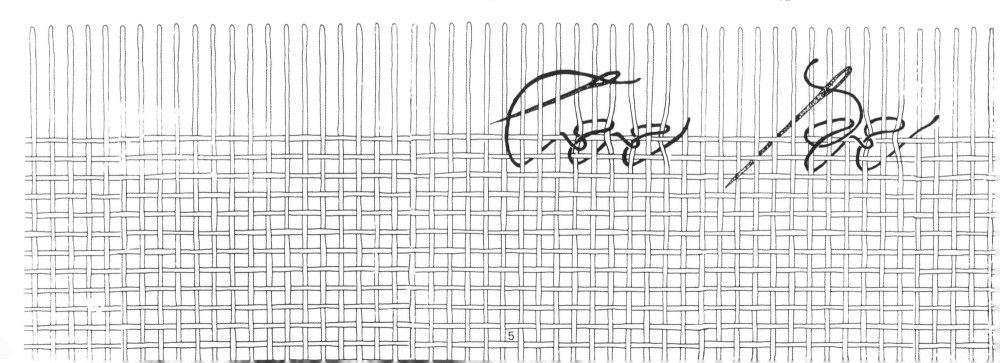

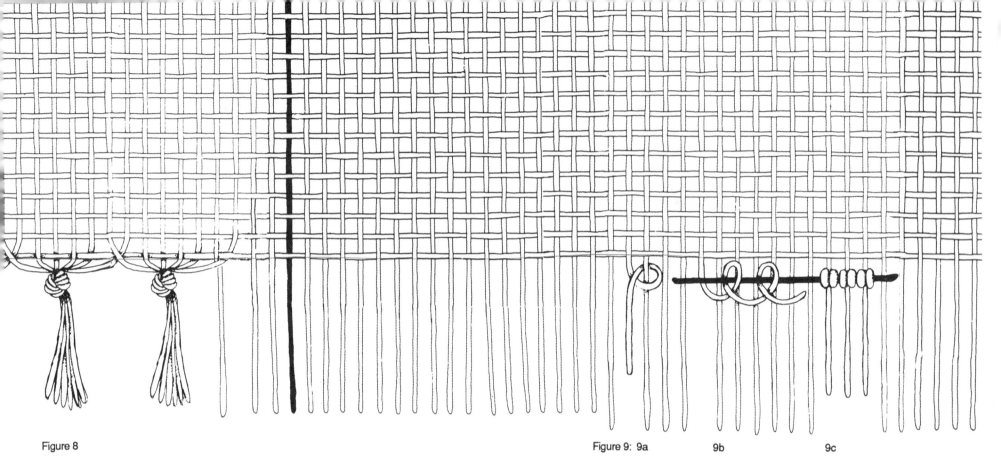

Figure 8

Figure 9: 9a   9b   9c

OVERHAND KNOTS

The Overhand Knot is the most widely known and used knotted weft protector. As weft protectors go, this one is lumpy and difficult to get close to the edge. It is often overused as a finish to weaving and should only be used after careful thought. One hint given by Collingwood is to *cross the warp ends before knotting* (fig. 8). Complete instructions for making the overhand knot can be found on page 13.

HALF-HITCH EDGINGS

A number of knotted edgings are made with *Half-Hitch knots*. Experiment with all of the half-hitch protectors by working successive rows from the same direction and by turning the fabric over on alternate rows to reverse the direction. Interesting textures result. In fact, you may find yourself wanting to do a complete piece in one of these knotting techniques!

Horizontal Half-Hitch Edge

This Half-Hitch variation may be used to advantage on a fairly dense warp. It produces a *beaded edge*.

Figure 9a shows a simple Half-Hitch. *The knotting proceeds from left to right, and the motion is **over, under and down***. In 9b, an additional yarn is stretched taut across the warp (it may be pinned in place), and each warp end repeats the knotting motion twice around this holding cord. Figure 9c shows the result.

6

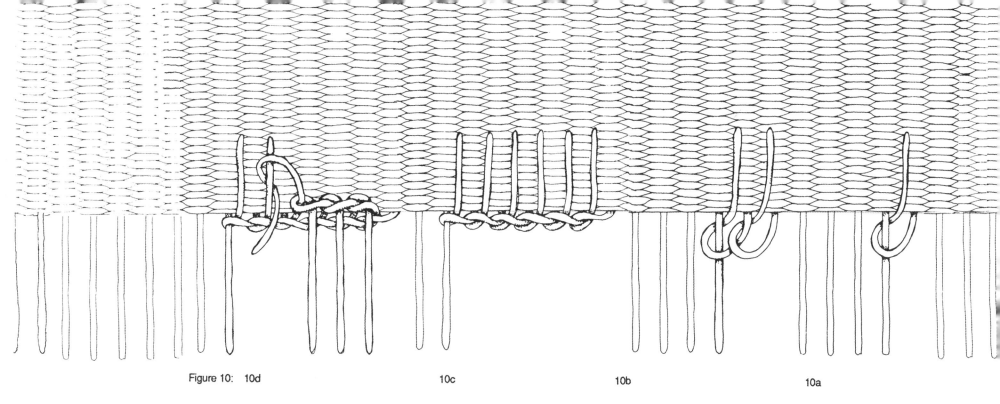

Figure 10: 10d   10c   10b   10a

Note: The knotting of the Damascus Edge proceeds from right to left.

Damascus Edge

The Damascus Edge is a good finish for thick warp. Half-hitch knots are worked around passive warp ends by active warp ends (fig. 10). *Working from right to left, hold the passive warp end in your left hand and the active warp end in your right hand. The knotting motion is:* **over, under, and up**. *The last active warp end finishes in a vertical position above the fringe (fig. 10a). Drop this warp end. Transfer the passive warp end to your right hand; it becomes the active warp end. With your left hand, pick up the next free warp end, a new passive warp end. Now repeat the knotting motion* (fig. 10b). One warp is always left at the edge after all warps have been knotted (fig. 10c).

Once all of the warp ends (except the last one) are in position above the fringe line, they may be worked down from the top following the same method (fig. 10d). Or, the warp ends may simply be brought down and knotted again from right to left. A third alternative is to turn the fabric over and knot from the other side. By alternating sides in this way, the effect of the knotted edge going off at an angle is counteracted.

Plate 15 shows a single row of Damascus Edge used as a foundation for weaving the warp ends back into the cloth in a contemporary Swedish tapestry.

7

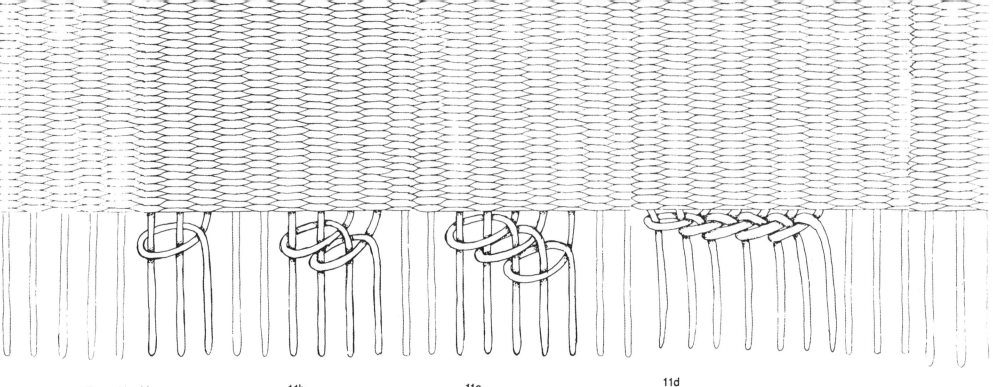

Figure 11: 11a   11b   11c   11d

Philippine Edge

One of our favorite weft protectors, the Phillipine Edge, is shown in figure 11. It is used frequently on weft-faced fabrics, such as rugs, and on the rims of baskets. Plate 3 shows it used on a warp-faced fabric as well (on a Mexican textile)! it is a very versatile edging, producing a neat, braided look. *Work this edging from left to right. Hold the first two warp ends (the passive ones) in your left hand, and the third warp end (the active one) in your right hand. Wrap the active end around the passive ones* (fig. 11a).

*The knotting motion is: **over, under and down.** Drop the warp end farthest to the left. Transfer the right-hand warp end to your left hand; it now becomes passive. Then pick up a new active warp end with the right hand. Repeat the knotting motion (fig. 11b).* Continue as in figure 11c and d.

As with the other half-hitch edgings, the Philippine Edge may be worked row after row on the same side or from alternate sides of the fabric.

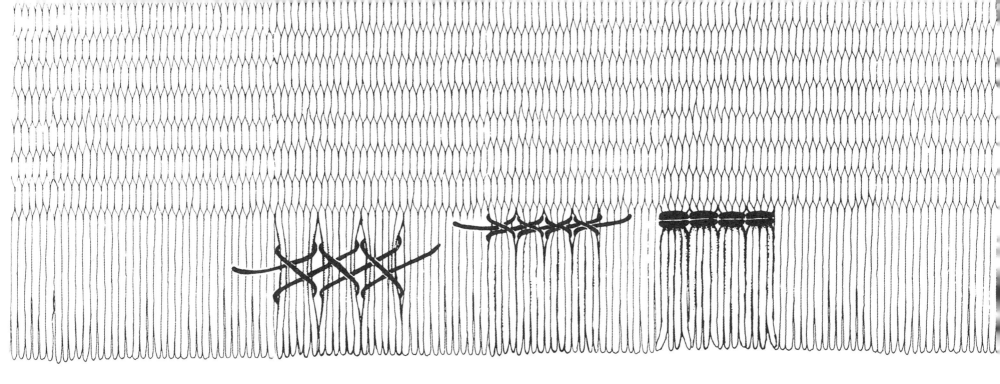

Figure 12: 12a   12b   12c

Neolithic Edge

An excellent finish for warp-faced textiles has been named the Neolithic Knot by Mary Atwater. Macrame enthusiasts are familiar with the reverse side of this knot, the Vertical Half-Hitch. Each side of the knot has a distinct personality, and either may be exploited for its decorative potential (figs. 12a,b). Figure 12c shows the reverse side of the knot.

To start, select groups of warp ends to knot around. You may have to experiment with different sized groups for the right look. *A separate strand of yarn is knotted around each group of warps. Work from left to right in a figure-eight fashion. Lay the wrapping yarn over the first group of warp ends. Wrap it around the first group, diagonally across the top of it, then under it once again. Bring the end of the wrapping yarn underneath the top diagonal. You are now in position to wrap the next group of warp ends.*

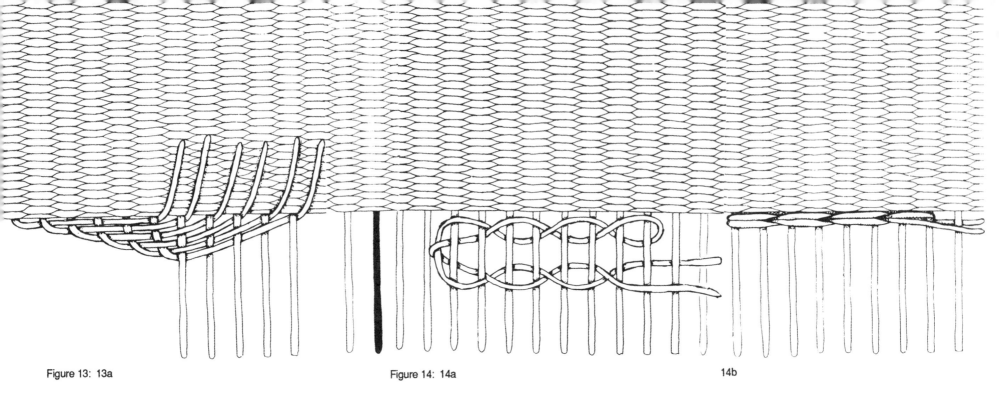

Figure 13: 13a

Figure 14: 14a

14b

Woven Weft Protectors

WOVEN EDGE

The Woven Edge, diagrammed in figure 13, is often found on Scandinavian rugs. The weaving of the warp ends may begin in the center of the piece, as in figure 13b, or at one edge, as in figure 13c.

Weave the first warp end under and over neighboring warp ends for a given distance. Lay it above the fell line. Then weave the second warp end across the same number of warp ends as the first one. A diagonal is formed at the edge. The warp ends extending above the fell line may be trimmed off after weaving is complete.

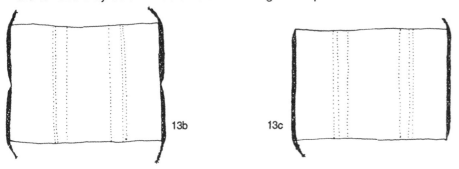

13b

13c

Bound Weft Protectors

With Bound weft protectors, an additional yarn is used to *encircle* warp ends, to hold the weft in place.

TWINING

While complete textiles can be made with twining techniques, twining can also be an effective weft protector. Single heavy warp ends or groups of fine warps can be encircled by the twining. See figure 14a and b. Navajo weavers traditionally use twining at the four selvage edges of their blankets. See plate 24 for an example.

An additional yarn is used to twine. Double it and enfold the first group of warp ends. Then exchange the position of the top and bottom twining strands. Experimenting with the way in which strands are twined will give you different texture and /or color patterns.

10

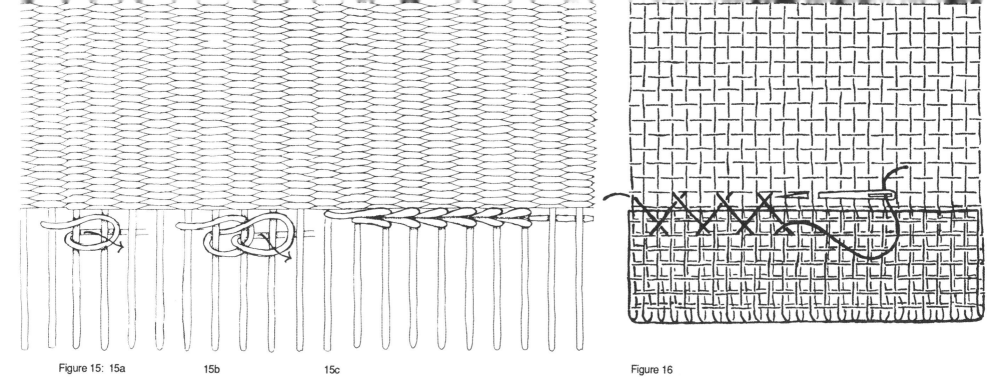

Figure 15: 15a   15b   15c

Figure 16

Sewn Weft Protectors

CHAINING
Chaining is also done with a supplemental thread, and can encircle single heavy warp threads or groups of finer warp. It is the same process as *crochet*, and can be done with a hook or with the fingers. See figure 15.

Lay the supplemental thread underneath the warp. Form a loop at the edge (fig. 15a). *Draw up a new loop through this first loop after each warp end or groups of warps* (fig. 15b). Continue looping across as in figure 15c.

By sewn weft protectors, we mean *hems*, either functional or decorative.

HERRINGBONE HEM
The Herringbone Stitch is worked from left to right as in figure 16. *Take a small stitch into the fabric and another small stitch below, on the hem. Note that the stitches progress from left to right, while the needle is always moving from right to left.*

The stitches of the hem "give," making it a good choice for hemming heavy fabrics or knits.

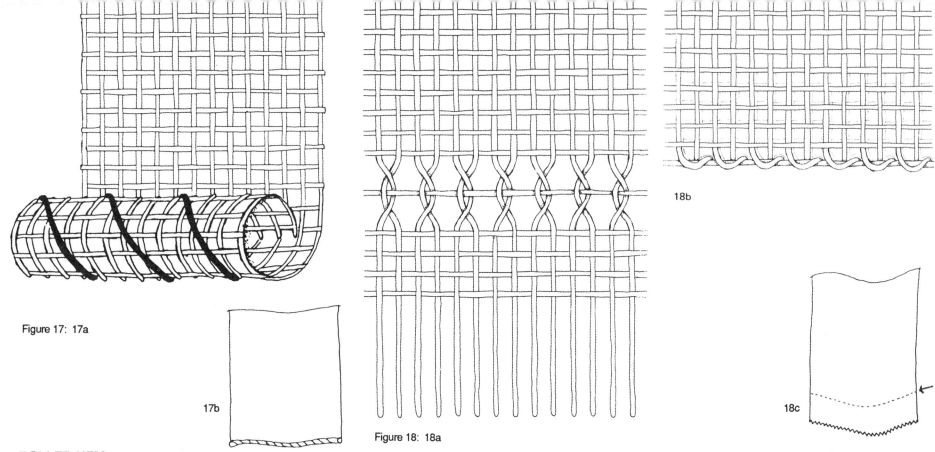

Figure 17: 17a

17b

Figure 18: 18a

18b

18c

ROLLED HEM

Figure 17 shows one possibility for stitching a Rolled Hem. Many decorative effects can result from the manner of stitching.

Roll the fabric tightly and stitch as for overcasting (fig. 5, page 4). This hem is excellent for fine fabrics. It may be too bulky for thicker handwovens.

Decorative stitching on a rolled hem is shown on plate 21.

PICOT HEM

This hem takes some on-loom planning.

Figure 18 shows how a row of *leno* woven at the hemline of a fabric will create a *picot edge* when the hem is folded at that point. The leno cross is shown in figure 18a. Figures 18b and c show the picot edge at the foldline.

Planning for Hems

Here are a few on-loom hints to keep in mind if you are making placemats, clothing or other items which might require a hem.

A fine sewing thread may be woven along the line where the fold of the hem will be. It stands out and can be used as a guideline for the fold.

Many weavers recommend the use of *finer yarn* for weaving the hem portion of a project, to reduce its bulk.

Be sure to *stitch along one weft thread* when stitching the hem in place, to keep the stitches from showing.

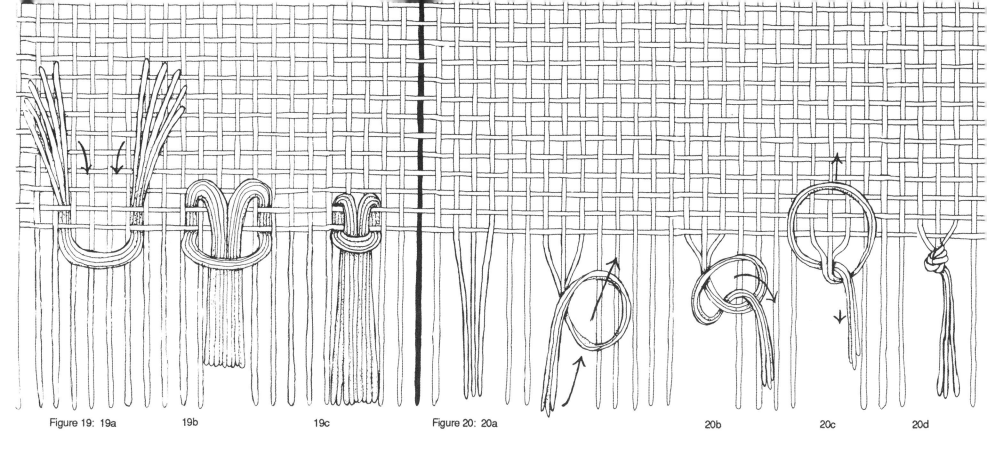

Figure 19: 19a   19b   19c   Figure 20: 20a   20b   20c   20d

Part II
Warp Protectors

The warp protectors consist primarily of *fringe treatments and braids*, which keep the fringe ends of a piece from unravelling. They may be divided into the following classes: *Knotted, Braided, Woven, Twisted, Wrapped.* Naturally, all of the material in this section has relevance beyond warp protection. Many of these techniques will be useful as trims as well.

Note that *an entire piece may be created out of fringes.* The grass skirts of the Samoans, the mantles of the Maori, and the wrapped forms of Sheila Hicks are all good examples.

Allowance for take-up in the warp protectors should be planned for before the weaving. Overhand knots take up about one inch of warp. Braids have 15-30% take-up. Be sure to allow enough fringe.

If fringe is needed, but wasn't planned for in the weaving, it may be added to the selvage or hemmed edges with *snitch knots*, or *larks head knots*, as shown in fig. 19.

Knotted Warp Protectors

OVERHAND KNOTS
Just as the Overhand Knot was the basic weft protector (see fig. 8, page 6), variations on the Overhand Knot are the basic warp protectors. Remember to be thoughtful in the use of any finish, but particularly the poor, overused overhand knot. Figure 20 shows the proper method of tying overhand knots.

13

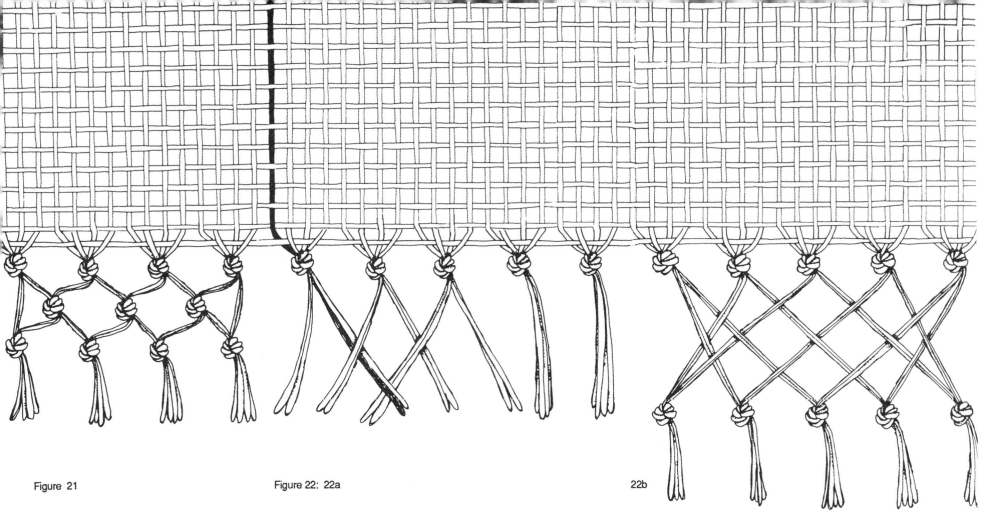

Figure 21   Figure 22: 22a   22b

Alternating Overhand Knots

Elaborate fringe treatments are worked in alternating overhand knots in textiles the world over. See plate 1 for a Turkish example. Outstanding examples can be seen in Mexican and Ecuadorian fine cotton shawls which have geometric designs and figures knotted into the fringes. Plate 12 shows such an edge on a Mexican shawl.

One row of Overhand Knots is made at the edge of the piece. Then, each group of warp ends is divided in half. Halves that are side-by-side are joined to form a new group to knot (fig. 21). A stick or ruler inserted between the rows of knots is a good way to space the work accurately.

Alternating, Interlaced Overhand Knots

This Overhand Knot variation makes a very lacy edging. In this version, *a few groups of warp ends are interwoven before a second row of knots is tied* (fig. 22). It takes a bit of practice, but if you follow the diagram and stick with it, you will have a very satisfying finish. Imagine it on a baby blanket or a shawl!

14

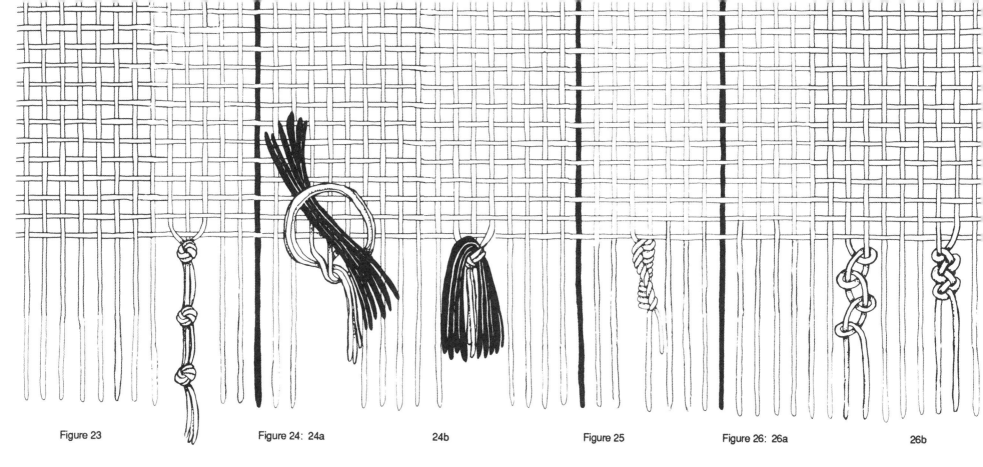

Figure 23   Figure 24: 24a   24b   Figure 25   Figure 26: 26a   26b

Overhand Knots in Succession
Tying *a series of knots*, in the same group of warp ends is a good way
to thicken a skimpy fringe (fig. 23).

Augmented Overhand Knots
Another good way to add fullness to a fringe is to *add a bundle of extra
yarns into the overhand knot* (fig. 24). The additional yarns may be of
one color or of many colors.

Plate 16 shows the use of Augmented Overhand Knots to add color
to the fringe of a textile from Cyprus.

HALF-HITCH KNOTS
The Half-Hitch variations provide us with several warp protectors. Most
of them have a thickening effect on sparse fringe. The Half-Hitch is
also discussed on page 6.

Vertical Half-Hitch
Successive Half-Hitch knotting of one warp end around another forms
a spiral and makes a thicker fringe (fig. 25). *One warp end is passive
and the other is active, wrapping itself continuously around the
passive end.*

Alternating Half-Hitch
Alternation of the Half-Hitches is shown in figure 26. *Hold one strand
in each hand. Knot first with the right hand, then with the left hand.
The strand that is not knotting should be held taut.*

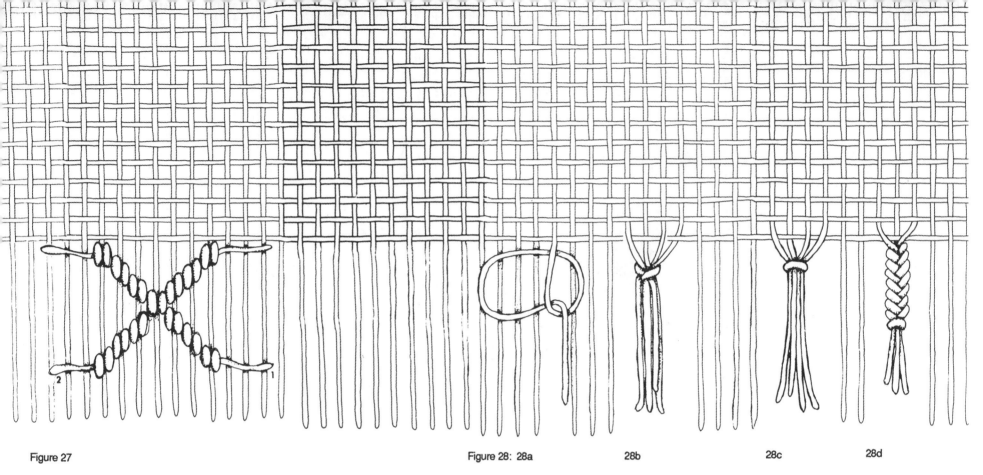

Figure 27

Figure 28: 28a   28b   28c   28d

Diagonal Half-Hitch

Figure 27 shows the method of forming Diagonal Half-Hitches. This is a finish often seen on woolen stoles from Mexico. It is a border treatment that appears elaborate, but is quick to do.

Hold end number 1 taut diagonally to the right and knot each of the other warp ends around it until the center of the x-shape is reached. Then hold end number 2 taut diagonally to the left and knot the other warp ends around it across the entire x-shape. Pick up end number 1 again and complete the motif.

Guided Half-Hitch

The Guided Half-Hitch provides a useful means of *grouping* warp ends. In macrame terms it is called the *gathering knot* and is illustrated in figure 28a and b. Figure 28c shows the reverse side of the knot.

This knot may be used in place of overhand knots in the alternating overhand knot edging. It has the advantage of not being lumpy and bumpy; it lies flat. It is not a tight knot, so with slippery material it may not be very secure. However, with wool and other fibers with some grip, it is quite satisfactory. Plate 7 shows the Guided Half-Hitch on the border of a Mexican shawl. The Guided Half-Hitch is a useful knot for the ends of braids, also (fig. 28d).

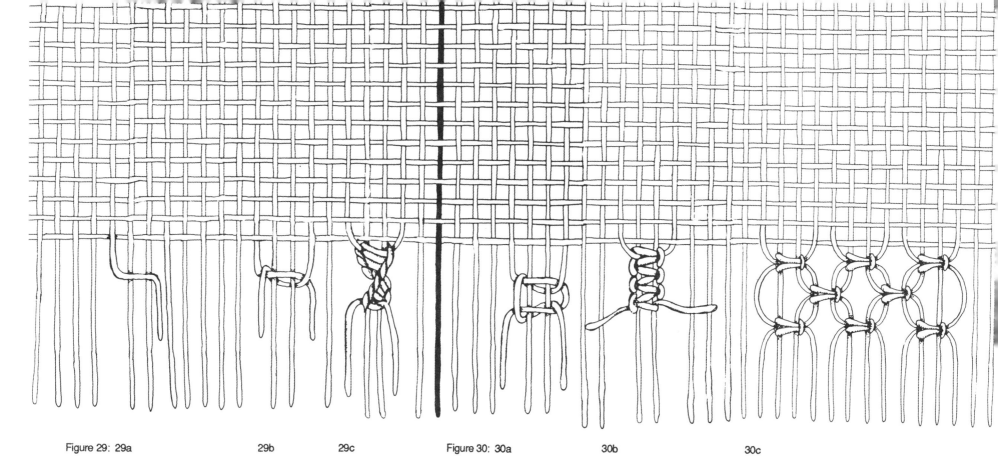

Figure 29: 29a   29b   29c   Figure 30: 30a   30b   30c

SQUARE KNOTS
The various uses for the Square Knot also provide us with several warp protectors.

Half Knot Sennits
The braid-like effect of sennits has a thickening effect on fringes. The Half Knot Sennit forms a spiral.

The two center strands are passive. There are two active strands, one for the left hand and one for the right hand. *To make the knot, place the left-hand strand across the passive strands (fig. 29a). Then place the right-hand strand **over** the left hand strand. Bring the right-hand strand **under** the passive strands and up into the loop formed by the left-hand strand (fig. 29b). Repeating* these knotting motions will form a spiral around the passive strand core (fig. 29c).

Square Knot Sennits
Providing the mirror image of the Half Knot completes the Square Knot to form a sennit which lies flat. *Begin as for the Half Knot (fig. 20a and b). Then turn the right-hand strand across the passive strands. Bring the left-hand strand **under** the passive strands and **up** through the loop (fig. 30a). Repeating the square knot produces a sennit (fig. 30b).*

Alternating Square Knot
Figure 30c shows the Square Knots in alternation. It is a very lacy way to finish a piece. *Here, the passive warp ends of one row become the active warp ends of the next row.*

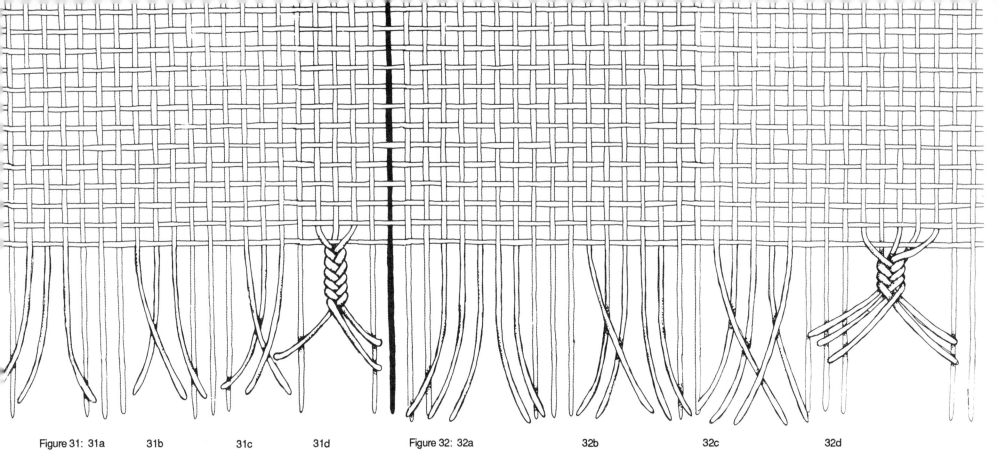

Figure 31: 31a   31b   31c   31d   Figure 32: 32a   32b   32c   32d

Braided Warp Protectors

Don't let those warp ends just sit there, braid them! Several strands of warp may comprise one strand of a braid. Once a series of braids is finished, they may be interlaced to further elaborate the finish. Small braids may be joined to form larger braids, then split off again. Braids may also be matched to stripes in the warp. Imagine a wide braid on a wide stripe next to a narrow braid on a narrow stripe. We have space here to mention only a few basic braids. For others, see the Barker book and Marsten article listed in the bibliography. There are two types of braids--*flat* and *round*.

All of the braids in this section may be used for added-on trims as well as for warp protectors. *Be sure to keep the braiding strands under tension, so that the resulting product will be firm and even.*

End all braids with the Gathering Knot, shown in figure 28, page 16; or with *Wrapping,* shown in figure 41, page 24.

FLAT BRAIDS
Three-Strand Flat Braid
The Three-Strand Braid is the most familiar flat braid. It is the braid most people use when they braid their hair. See figure 31.
For variation, try using yarns of different sizes in the braid. Two thick yarns and one thin one produce an interesting effect.

Two strands are held in the left hand, one strand in the right hand (fig. 31a). *Bring the outer left strand across to the opposite side* (fig. 31b). *Now there are two strands in the right hand, one in the left. Cross the outer right strand over to the left side* (fig. 31c).

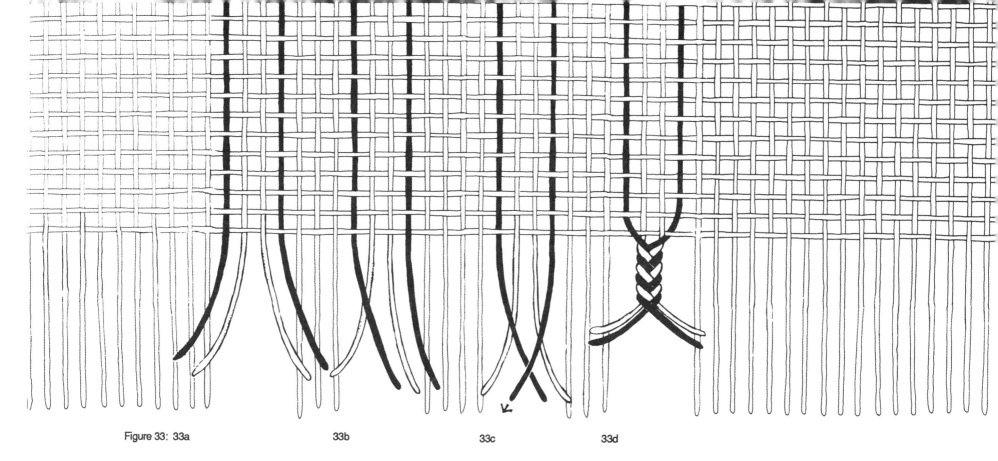

Figure 33: 33a   33b   33c   33d

Five-Strand Flat Braid
Closely related to the Three-Strand Braid, the Five-Strand Braid is executed in a similar fashion, with *outside strands brought to the center* (fig. 32). The resulting braid has a bias character to it, broader and more interesting than the three-strand braid. It would be a nice trim for a garment, following the curve of a neckline, for example. Try the same method using seven or nine strands.

Four-Strand Flat Braid
As with all braids, this one can be done with strands all in one color, or with different color arrangements. One of our favorite arrangements is in dark, light, light, dark order. The resulting braid takes on an arrow pattern.

Like the other flat braids, it is worked by *bringing an outside thread across to the opposite side*. Figure 33 shows the movement of the strands from the outside to the center. The completed braid is shown in figure 33d.

Four-strand flat braids have been used to decorate the fringes of some old Norwegian textiles in an elaborate grouping, separating and regrouping process called *firfletting*. See plate 14 for an example.

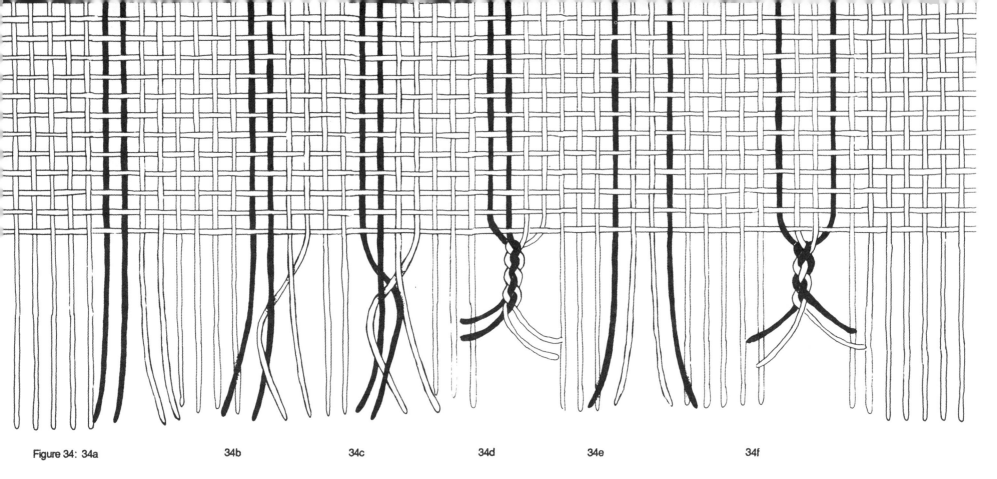

Figure 34: 34a   34b   34c   34d   34e   34f

ROUND BRAIDS
Four-Strand Round Braid
The Four-Strand Round Braid is widely used in ethnic textiles. The method of working is shown in figure 34.

Begin with two strands in each hand (fig. 34a). *Bring the outer right strand **under** the next two strands, then back **over** one* (fig.34b). In other words, the right-hand strand returns to its "own side." It is now the *innermost* strand on the right. *The same action is now repeated with the outer left strand, **under two, back over one*** (fig. 34c). The completed braid is shown in figure 34d.

It is fun to experiment with color sequences in this braid, also. Try arranging the warp ends in light, light,m dark, dark order. Then try the braid with the colors in an alternating order: dark, light, light, dark, as in figure 34e. The first version will have vertical stripes, and the second will have candycane-type diagonal stripes (fig. 34f). Choose the effect that best complements your textile.

If you are trying out all of the four strand braid variations on the same group of yarns, make a Gathering Knot between each type so you can rearrange the colors.

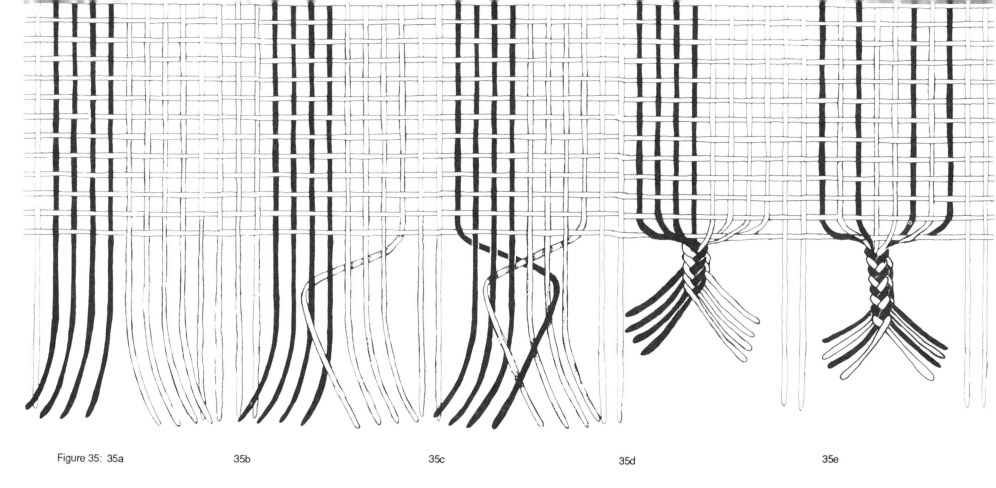

Figure 35: 35a   35b   35c   35d   35e

Eight-Strand Round Braid

The Eight-Strand Braid shown in figure 35 is an elaboration of the Four-Strand braiding technique. *Work with four strands in each hand* (fig. 35a). *Bring the outermost strand on the right* **under** *five strands,* **up** *through the center of the opposite group, then back to its "own side"* (fig. 35b). *It is now the innermost strand on the right. The braiding motion is "under five, back over two." Repeat this motion with the outermost strand on the left* (fig. 35c). Figure 35d shows the completed braid.

It is easier to learn the Eight-Strand Braid if you use four light-colored threats in one hand and four dark ones in the other hand. Then, after you have mastered it that way, try alternating the colors in a mirror image as shown in figure 35e.

As in the Four-Strand braids, two different designs appear with the two different color arrangements. Plate 18 shows eight-strand braids used on the fringe of a Turkish bag.

An Eight-Strand braid can be divided into two Four-Strand braids, round or flat, and these can then be recombined. When worked very tightly in heavy yarns, this sturdy braid makes an excellent bag handle.

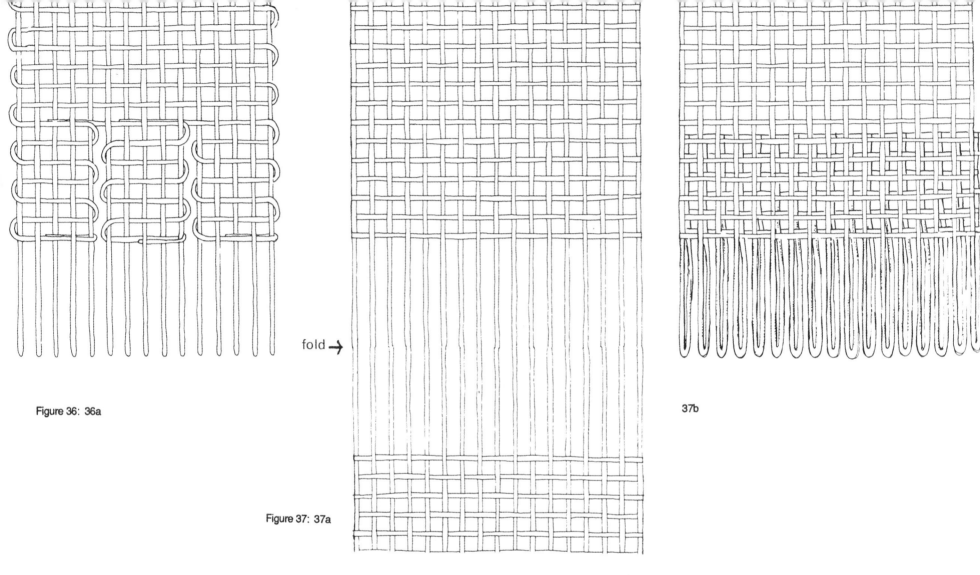

fold →

Figure 36: 36a

Figure 37: 37a

37b

Woven Warp Protectors

TABS

Woven *Tab Fringes* are fun to try for an on-loom finish. *A separate shuttle or strand of weft is needed for each tab.* See figure 36. The ancient Peruvians used woven tabs a great deal to decorate their garments. Plates 28 and 32 show two styles of tabs used in ancient Peruvian textile fragments.

WOVEN FRINGE
Warp Fringe

Another on-loom finish is a *Woven Fringe* for projects that are to be hemmed, as shown in figure 37.

Weave the hem, *leave open warp between the hem and the main body of the piece*, then weave the piece (fig. 37a). When the project is finished, sew the hem to the cloth. The open warp area becomes a looped fringe (fig. 37b). The loops work especially well for preserving ravelly yarn.

22

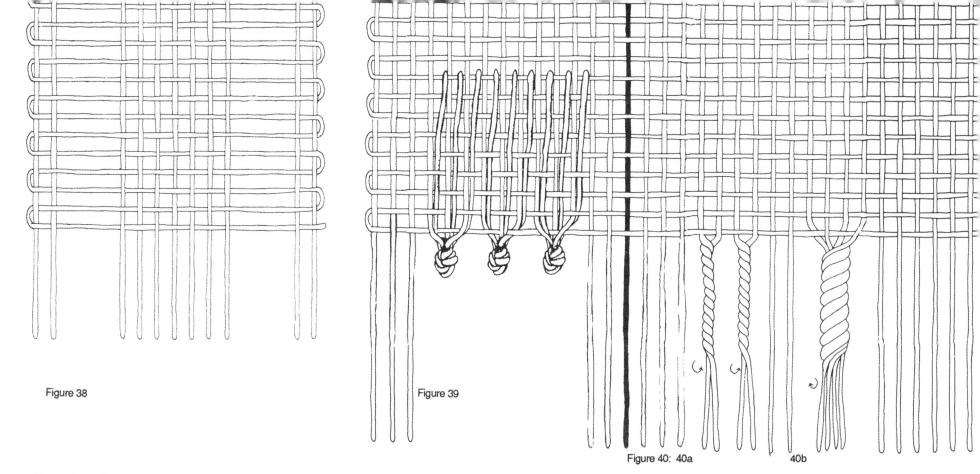

Figure 38

Figure 39

Figure 40: 40a   40b

Non-Warp Fringe

We should mention non-warp fringes also. Fringe may be woven at the *selvage edges* of a piece as well. See figure 38 for an example of selvage fringe being woven on the loom. Note that *two scaffold or "dummy" warp threads* are placed the desired distance from the body of the piece to provide an even fringe. These are pulled out or cut off when the weaving is completed. (If a slippery material is used in the weaving, a second weft could be used in the body of the piece only, to keep its selvages from slipping into the fringe area.)

WEAVING IN ENDS

Needleweaving the warp ends to work them back into the cloth is an alternative when a perfectly plain edge is desired. This is not really as time consuming as it sounds, and is a very crisp, clean finish. Refer to figure 3, page 3. Weaving in warp ends after overhand knots have been tied produces a *picot edge effect* (fig. 39).

Plied Warp Protectors

TWISTING

Warp ends may be Twisted or Plied, as shown in figure 40. *Take two groups of warp ends and twist them in the same direction* (fig. 40a). *When they are twisted so tightly that they begin to kink, place the two groups together and twist them in the opposite direction* (fig. 40b). *Knot the ends together.*

The ends of a wool warp may be *felted* by holding them over the spout of a steaming teakettle. This eliminates the need to knot, and the ends will not unravel if trimmed.

Twisted fringe lends a handsome finish to blankets and hangings, and is well worth the time involved. Plate 20 shows twisted fringe used as a decorative finish on a Norwegian headscarf.

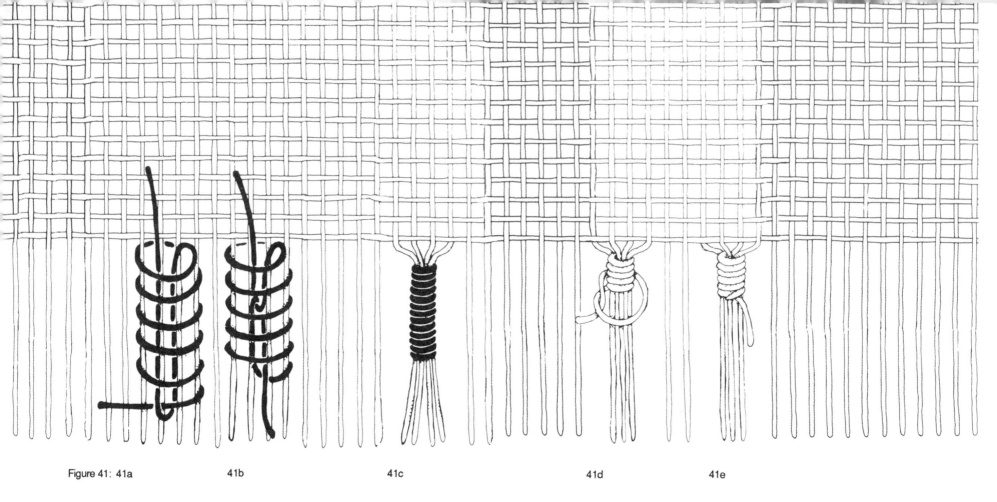

Figure 41: 41a   41b   41c   41d   41e

Bound Warp Protectors

WRAPPING

You may wish to try *Wrapping* or *Whipping* warp ends as a means of binding them tightly in place, or of forming long, slender coils (fig. 41). *Form a u-shape with one end of the wrapping strand and wind firmly over it and the bundle of warp with the other end, from top to bottom* (fig. 41a). *Insert the end of the wrapping strand into the loop of the "u" and pull on the top end to lock the wrapping on* (fig. 41b). *Trim off ends.* The completed wrapping is shown in figure 41c. Figures 41d and e show wrapping secured with a gathering knot.

Plates 4 and 4a show wrapping in many colors used as a decorative trim at the bottom of a Bolivian coca bag.

Wrapping is an excellent means of adding feathers to a piece. But don't forget to think of the total piece. Add feathers only if it will enhance the total impression you are trying to create.

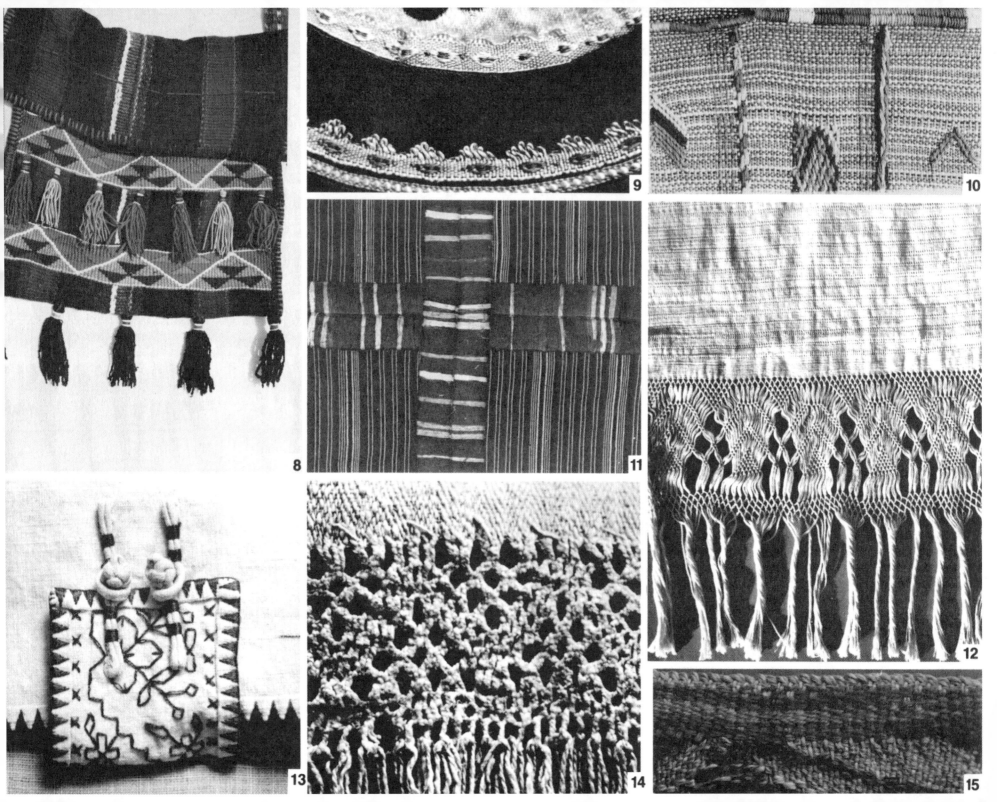

25

26

27

28

29

30

31

32

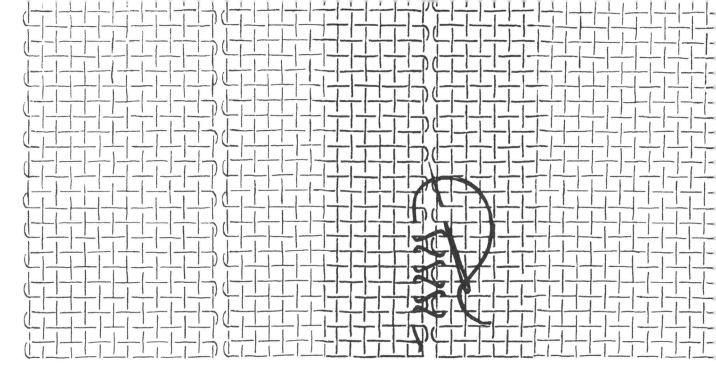

Figure 42

Part III:
Joins

Where two pieces of fabric come together, joins may either camouflage or draw attention to this merger. Joins can be *stitched, woven or crocheted*.

The question of whether or not to use a sewing machine always arises when joins of any kind are considered. We refer to our earlier statements about the overall effect you are trying to create. If a sewing machine will not detract from your goal, use it. If it will strengthen a piece that needs strengthening, use it. But if machine stitches will detract from your beautiful handwork, then, by all means, use hand techniques.

Direct Joins

The decorative joins presented here make use of embroidery stitches to enhance the lines of the join. Some are worked as *direct joins*; that is, they are the only stitches necessary to hold the two cloths together. Others, the *decorative joins*, are less strong, and are used to embellish already-sewn seams. Using yarn of a contrasting color will enhance the decorative effects of these joining stitches.

LOOPING
For an invisible join, *simple Looping through selvage loops* will draw two pieces of fabric together (fig. 42). This is the same stitch that is used to sew sweaters together.

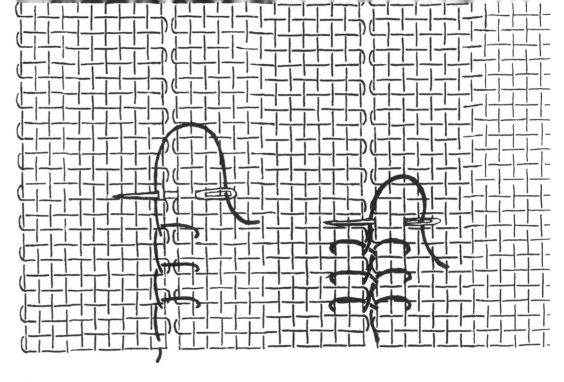

Figure 43: 43a   Figure 44: 44a   44b

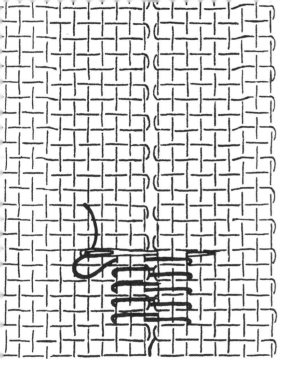

43b   44c

FIGURE-EIGHT STITCH

A straightforward way of joining fabrics is with Figure-Eight stitches *worked very closely together*. Two ridges are produced in this manner (fig. 43). Plate 10 shows a Figure-Eight join used on a Guatemalan garment.

BUTTONHOLE STITCH

The Buttonhole Stitch can be used in many variations to produce subtle or bold lines. It is a reversible stitch, appearing much the same on both sides. The stitch, shown in figure 44a, is *worked from the right-hand fabric into the left-hand fabric*. The Buttonhole stitch is also discussed on page 4. Plate 19 shows the buttonhole stitch used to join the yoke to the body of a Mexican blouse.

Guatemalan skirts feature an interesting variation on the Buttonhole stitch, shown in figure 44b, wherein the stitch is worked first on one side of the seam, then on the opposite side. A braid-like ridge is formed in the center. Plate 11 and the cover photo show this variation on the Buttonhole stitch.

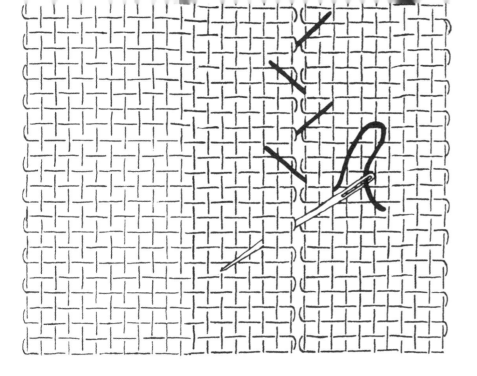

Figure 45: 45a

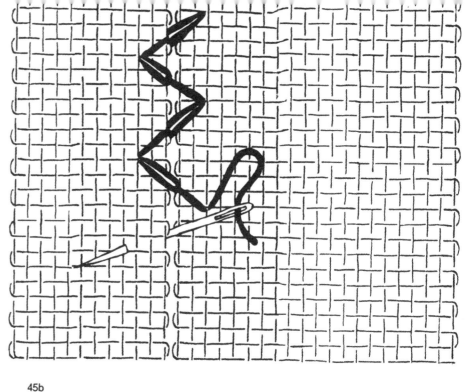

45b

Ancient Stitch

The Ancient Stitch, familiar to all owners of baseballs as the *Baseball Stitch*, is another useful method of joining pieces of fabric. Several variations are possible. It is a reversible stitch and may be inconspicuous or decorative. *Insert the needle between the two pieces to be joined, and into the cloth from underneath* (fig. 45a). Shoes are laced in this fashion.

45c

If you wish to make the *herringbone variation* shown in figure 45b, *work over the seam twice on each side.*

A Bolivian variation on the Ancient Stitch involves traversing the same course with the needle *three times* before going on to the next stitch.

Plates 2 and 27 show the Ancient Stitch used on Peruvian and Turkish textiles.

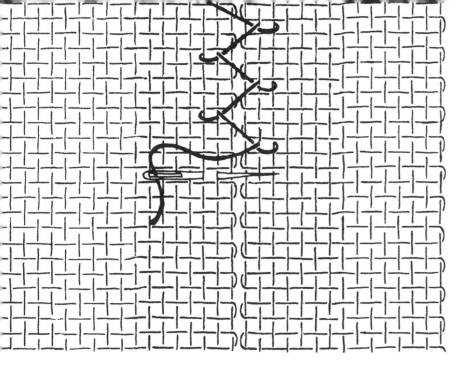

Figure 46: 46a

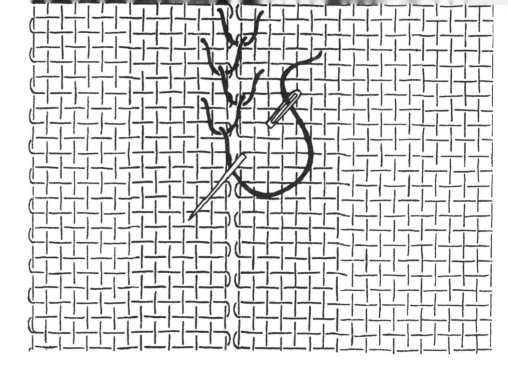

Figure 47: 47a

Decorative Joins

The following stitches are not strong in themselves, and are not reversible. They are best when worked over sewn seams for decoration.

CRETAN STITCH
Cretan Stitch is often exploited for its decorative potential. *Take tiny stitches perpendicular to the seam in a zigzag pattern* (fig. 46).

FEATHER STITCH
Figure 47 shows the highly decorative Feather Stitch. *Make larger stitches into the cloth on a diagonal. The bottom of the diagonal is aligned with the top of the preceding stitch.*

Plate 29 shows the feather stitch used to trim the seams of a Mexican shirt.

46b

47b

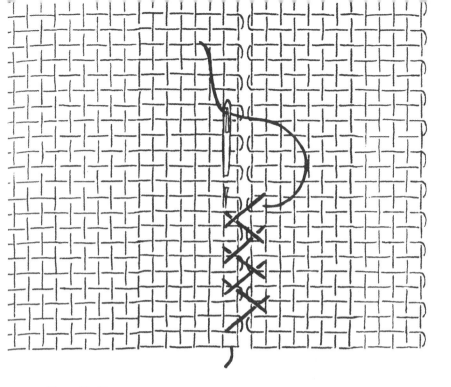

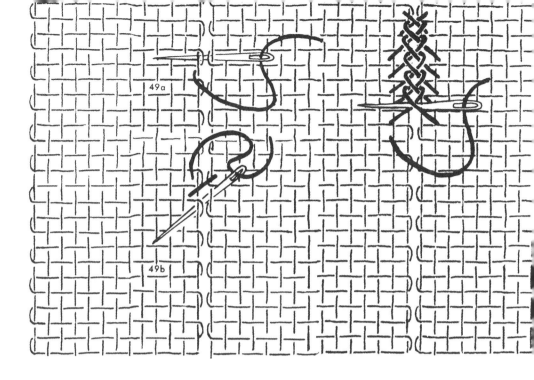

Figure 48: 48a

Figure 49:   49c

HERRINGBONE STITCH

Decorative uses for the Herringbone Stitch are shown in figure 48a and b. *Make tiny cross stitches on each side of the join.* Use of the Herringbone Stitch for hems is discussed on page 11.

Plate 30 shows Herringbone Stitch used as a decorative join on a pair of Eskimo mittens from Canada.

48b

VANDYKE STITCH

The VanDyke Stitch is both functional and decorative, and has great versatility (fig. 49).

Begin the stitch with a small cross over the seam (fig. 49a). *Then follow the diagram, inserting the needle right under the cross, into the stitch, not into the cloth* (fig. 49b,c).

Very tiny stitches worked close together create a *small ridge*. If VanDyke stitch is worked over the edges of a piece such as a bag, or on a seam with wrong sides together, a *braided ridge effect* is created (fig. 49c). This variation is sometimes called *cross-knit looping*, and we have seen it used in Bolivian and East European textiles. Plate 26 shows a Bolivian example.

49d

49e

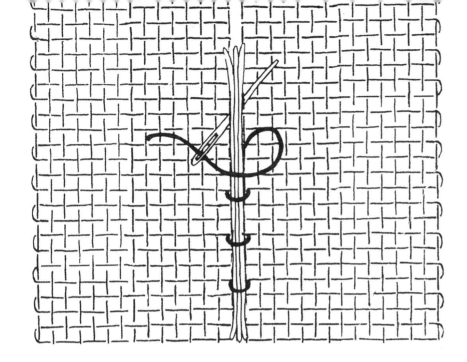

Figure 50: 50a

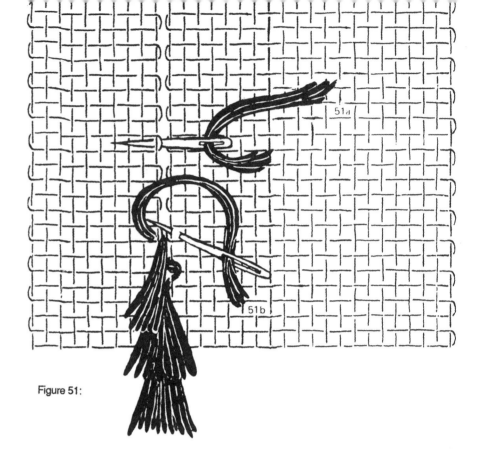

Figure 51:

COUCHING

Couching will disguise a seam effectively. Place yarns harmonious with the piece in the seam, perhaps the warp yarn. It may be just enough to fill the small crevice created by the seam, or more for a fluffier effect. Stitch over these with a second yarn, perhaps the weft yarn (fig. 50). This is a good use for thrums.

RYA KNOTS

Rya Knotting is another seam disguise. This, of course, would be highly decorative as well. It would draw attention to the area that has been concealed. Figure 51 shows the method of working the knots *from the bottom up. Always insert the needle in the same direction--from right to left.*

50b

51c

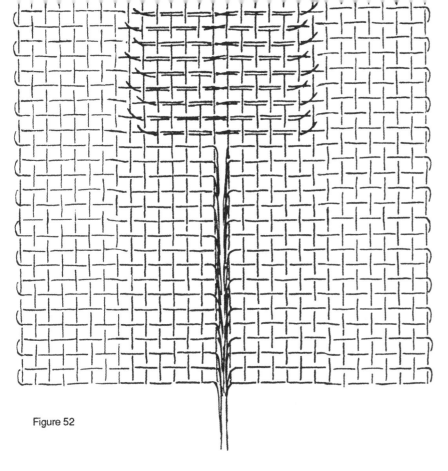

Figure 52

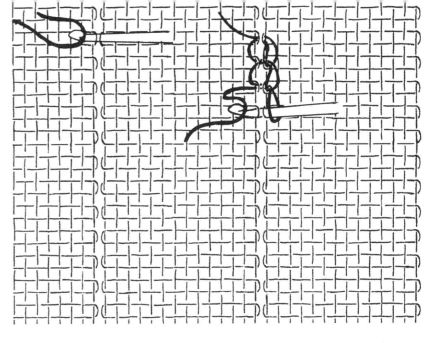

Figure 54: 54a   54b

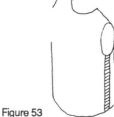

Figure 53

54c

Woven Joins

Needleweaving and Band Weaving are the main techniques used for woven joins.

WEAVING WARP ENDS

An interesting way of joining two pieces of weaving at the fringed ends is to *needleweave the warp ends of each piece into the other piece*, for instance, at the shoulder seam of a shaped garment (fig. 52). For a join at the selvage sides, long strands of weft might be left at the sides of the weaving and used to weave into another piece. Or, long wefts might come from two pieces and be knotted together.

WOVEN BANDS AND INSERTS

Woven bands, *inkle, card-woven* or *finger-woven* may be used as a means of decoratively covering the join in two pieces of fabric. They may also be placed between the two pieces for additional width, as in a garment (fig. 53).

Crochet Joins

Crochet is a decorative way to join pieces of heavy fabric together. A crocheted join is shown in figure 54. Plate 31 shows an interesting crocheted join on a Greek jacket.

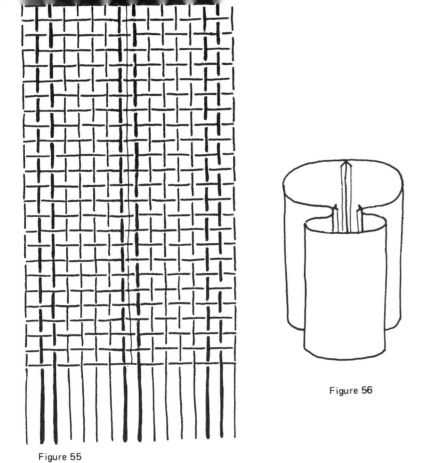

Figure 55

Figure 56

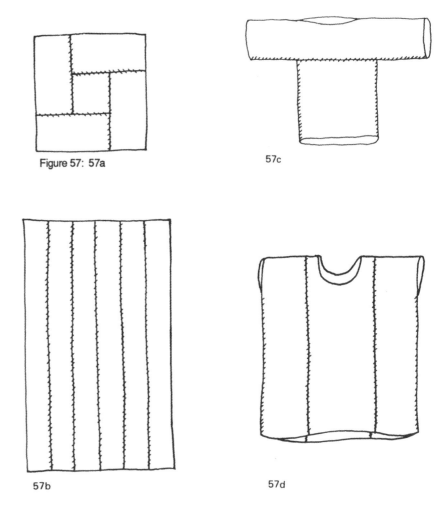

Figure 57: 57a

57c

57b

57d

Planning for Joins

Here are a few hints that you might wish to keep in mind to conceal seams when planning your weaving:

Occasional *heavy strands of yarn* can be placed throughout the warp
   so your seam will not be the only bulky area in the piece (fig. 55).
The seam can be located in a *concealed* place, for instance,
   under a pleat (fig. 56).

Figure 57 will give you some ideas on *joining small pieces of weaving to create larger shapes* for tablecloths, bedspreads, etc.
Many ethnic fabrics are composed of narrow pieces (woven on backstrap looms) that are joined to form larger units. Kente cloth, plate 23, is an example. Other examples can be seen in plates 2, 10, 11 and 27. The joins add a lovely decorative touch that is so appropriate for the piece as a whole. This should be the goal in using joins.

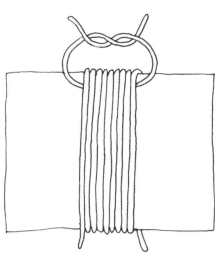

Figure 58: 58a

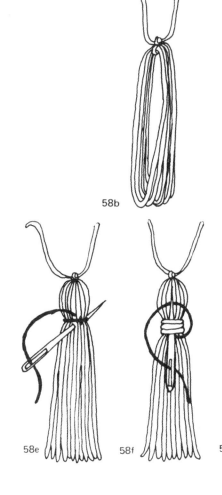

58b

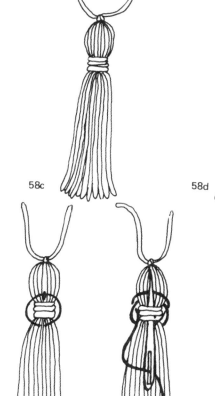

58c   58d

58e   58f   58g   58h   58i   58j

PART IV:
Embellishments

Embellishments are additions which should enrich your weaving. Certain materials are especially complimentary to weaving: leather, bone, wood, ceramic, horn, feathers, dull brass, copper, pewter and various beads. Use them whenever they are appropriate to the piece of weaving. We will discuss yarn embellishments here, which can be used in addition to, or instead of the above materials.

COMMON TASSEL
The most typical tassel is made over a piece of cardboard or heavy paper (fig. 58).

Wrap yarn around the cardboard for the desired thickness (fig. 58a). Don't be afraid to use an abundance of yarn. *Place an extra tying strand of strong yarn between the yarn bundle and the cardboard. Tie the bundle very tightly at one end* (fig. 58b). *Cut at the other end. Wrap the center section* (fig.58c). (Wrapping is shown on page 24.)

To make a fuller top, insert a *bead* before wrapping, (fig. 58d). Naturally, this would be for ornamental purposes. On garments, beads may beuncomfortable.

Many ethnic tassels are decorated with stitchery, needle looping or macrame. Stitching on tassels is shown in figure 58e-i. Plate 8 shows wrapped tassels added to an Israeli bag. Plates 17 and 18 show stitched tassels.

Figure 59: 59a   59b   59c   59d

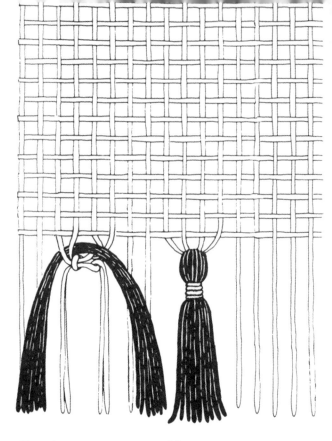

Figure 61: 61a   61b

Tassels may be added to the corners of pillows, or to the bottom of a bag. See figure 59a-c, and plate 17. *Tassels may also be worked into a braid.* See figure 59d, and the photo on the title page.

To make many tassels, you might employ a "production method." Set up clamps or posts and tie off tassels according to figure 60. Cut each bundle at the dotted line, fold at tie and wrap the top.

Figure 60

GUATEMALAN TASSELS

The Guatemalan tassel is particularly useful if you have a skimpy warp at the ends of your project and you want a nice, full finish. It can be worked close to the fabric for a rigid tasseled edge, or farther away from the fabric for "swinging" tassels.

Figure 61 shows the process for forming Guatemalan Tassels. *Tie a knot with groups of warp ends, then add extra yarn to form a tassel similar to those described on the preceding page.* The additional yarns could be the same as the warp yarn, or they might be of another color, so that the inside of the tassel would be the warp color, and the outside a contrasting color. Tassels in several colors are added to the borders of the Guatemalan shawl in plate 22.

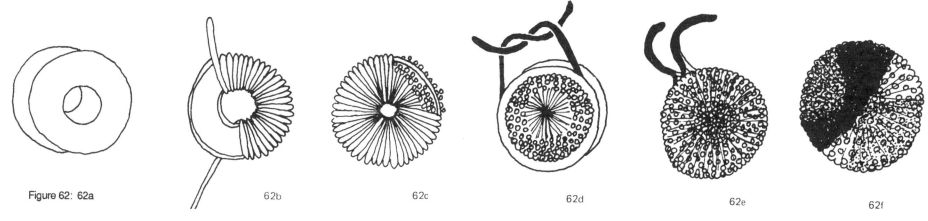

Figure 62: 62a   62b   62c   62d   62e   62f

Pom Poms

REGULAR POM-POMS

Pom-poms may be an important addition to many of your projects. For a regular pom-pom, you need to make *two round forms* out of cardboard or the plastic from bleach or detergent bottles. You may experiment with the size of these rounds, although the proportion between the inner and outer circles should be similar to that in figure 62a. Don't make the inner circle too large!

*Use a doubled strand of yarn to wrap over the **two** forms (fig. 62b). Continue wrapping with the yarn threaded on a needle until the inner circle is completley filled and it is necessary to poke through the center with the needle. Then insert the scissors **between the two forms** and cut all the way around the circle (fig. 62c). Before removing the forms, tie a strong yarn **very tightly** between the discs (fig. 62d). Finish with a nice clipping.* Figure 62e shows the completed pom-pom. Figure 62f shows a pom-pom made with three colors of yarn wound on the forms. The photo on page iii shows a pom-pom embellishment on a Turkish camel harness.

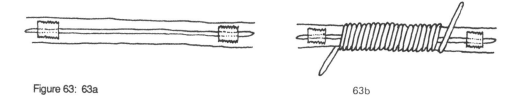

Figure 63: 63a   63b

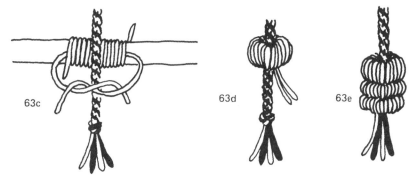

63c   63d   63e

BOLIVIAN POM-POMS

Three-layer Bolivian pom-poms are a delightful decoration. Figure 63 shows the procedure the making them. For a base, we use a size 8 knitting needle, although this varies with the size of the pom-pom and the thickness of the yarn.

Tape a six-inch piece of yarn to the knitting needle (fig. 63a). Wrap a second piece of yarn tightly around the needle about 30 times (fig. 63b). (This, too, will vary with the thickness of yarn used.) *Then,*

untape the short strand and tie its ends together around a braid or other core (fig. 63c), slipping the wrapped coil off the needle as you do so (fig. 63d). Make two more layers to complete the pom-pom (fig.63e). The Bolivians like to make the three layers in related colors for a rainbow effect. Plates 26 and 26a show the use of these pom-poms on a Bolivian coca bag.

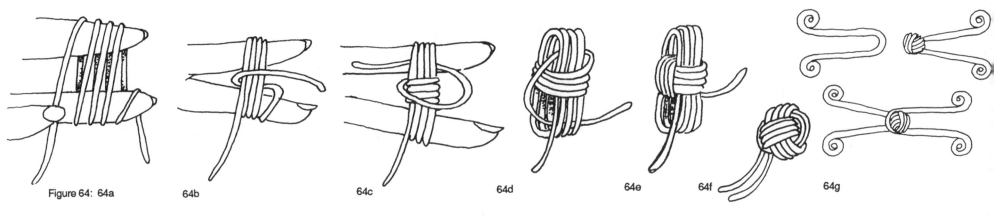

Figure 64: 64a   64b   64c   64d   64e   64f   64g

Buttons

MONKEY'S FIST

The Monkey's Fist is an oriental ball-like embellishment often used as a button. Aside from being quite a challenge to learn, it can be used decoratively, or as a button. Monkey's Fists are used in Chinese textiles as buttons in the "frog" closings of garments. Plates 6 and 13 show examples from Chinese garments.

The procedure is shown in figure 64a-f. Yarn is wound around the fingers in three different directions. *Wind first around two fingers* (fig. 64a), *then at right angles to the first wrapping,* (fig. 64b and c). At this point, a bead may be inserted for firmness. *Wrap in the third direction, at right angles to the second wrapping* (figs. 64d and e). *Long loops remain from the initial wrapping* (fig. 64e). *These loops are worked down toward the beginning, so that all the excess yarn comes out at the beginning end.* Figure 64f shows the completed button. Figure 64g shows a "frog" type of closing.

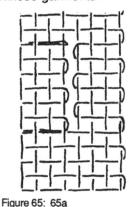 

Figure 65: 65a   65b

Buttonholes

SLITS

Ingenious ways of closing garments are frequently a problem for the weaver.

The most natural way to create buttonholes would be to *weave slits into the garment.* This might be done on the loom, as in figure 65a; or it could be done in a separate band which is then sewn to the garment, providing trim as well as a closing, as in figure 65b. Slits

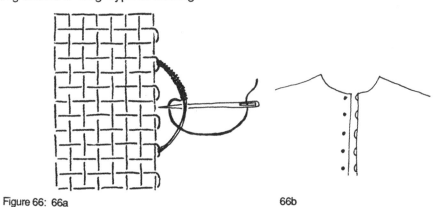

Figure 66: 66a   66b

might be bound with leather, or they might be reinforced with stitching, using yarn from the warp or weft.

LOOPS

Crocheted Cord Loops could serve as buttonholes (fig. 66). *The buttonhole stitch* may also be worked over a loop of yarn to form a button loop. Figure 6, page 4 shows how to work the buttonhole stitch.

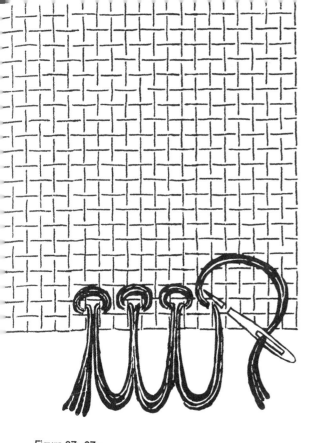

Figure 67: 67a

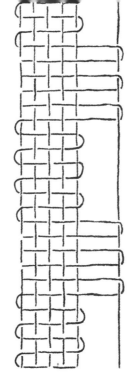

Figure 68: 68a

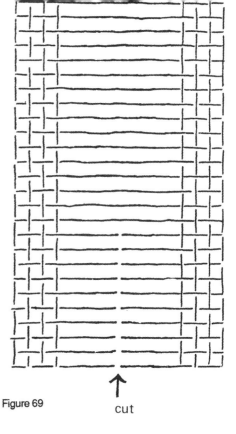

Figure 69   cut

Applied Fringe

ADDED YARN FRINGE

Additional yarn fringe may be applied to a selvage or a hemmed edge with *Snitch Knots*. See figure 19 page 13. *Rya Knots* may also be used to apply a fringe. Figure 67a shows applied rya knot fringe. *The knotting proceeds from left to right, while the needle always stitches from right to left.*

Figures 67b and c show some uses for applied fringes.

67b

67c

68b

WOVEN FRINGE

Do you ever have a few inches of warp left over at the end of a project? Why not use it to weave an inch or so of weft-faced fabric to be used as fringe on some future piece?

A *separate fringe* may be woven on the loom, or on an inkle, card or backstrap loom. This woven fringe may be applied to your bedspreads, clothing, etc. See figure 68. Plates 5 and 9 show this type of fringe applied to Peruvian and Chinese textiles.

A pattern may be woven into the fringe material, for instance, twill or overshot, or a patterned band weave.
Several fringes may be woven at once on wide looms and cut apart, as shown in figure 69.

41

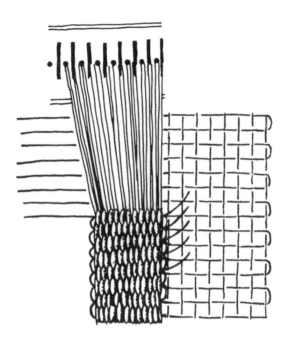

Figure 70

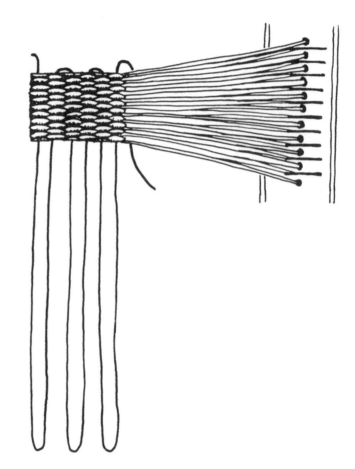

Figure 71

Woven Embellishments

FLAT BAND EDGING

A band may be woven onto the warp ends of a piece for a stunning woven band edge. Figure 70 shows how flat inkle or card woven bands can be "fused" to the edge of a fabric during the band weaving process by using the warp fringe of the fabric as weft in the band. This finish is most easily implemented when a backstrap method is used to weave the band.

Open a shed and lay in one or more of the fabric's warp ends.
Change the shed and beat. Weave the same fringe strand back
*   toward the fabric.*
Place a new fringe strand in this same shed.
Continue in this manner, weaving the previous fringe strand
*   back toward the fabric, and entering a new fringe weft in each*
*   shed. Trim all of the woven-in ends close to the fabric.*

Plate 25 shows a Bolivian flat band edging that is woven onto the four selvage edges of a manta.

The reverse of this finishing process was used in warp-weighted and sprang fabrics in Scandinavia as a heading for the warp in

warp-weighted weavings. A band was woven with long strands of weft pulled out from one edge (fig. 71). The piece was then turned sideways and lashed to the loom, the long weft strands becoming the weighted warp.

It is possible to use this method on a modern floor loom by lashing the band to the breast beam, threading the long wefts through the heddles and tying them at the back beam. After weaving the fabric, the remaining warp ends could be woven onto a band as in figure 70.

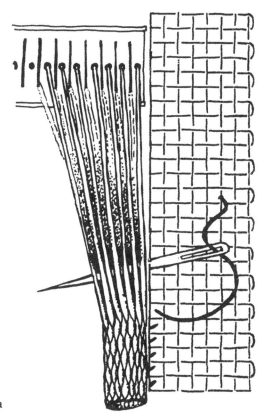

Figure 72: 72a

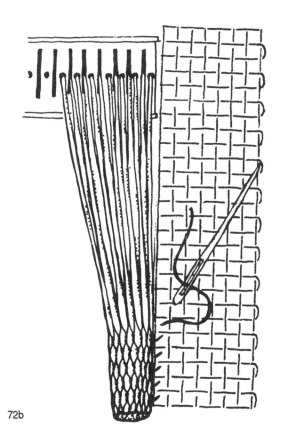

72b

TUBULAR BAND EDGING

A band can be *woven in a tubular fashion* by *always entering the weft from the same side and pulling tight.* One of our favorite Bolivian finishing techniques is a tubular band that is sewn on to the cloth, using the weft of the band to stitch and weave simultaneously! Figures 72a and b show the weaving/sewing on of a plain-weave tube. A tubular edging for a Bolivian Coca bag is shown in plate 26. Bolivian and Peruvian weavers do some astonishing pickup designs in their tubular bands while weaving and sewing them onto their coca bags and ponchos. The Cason and Cahlander book listed in the bibliography gives some detailed instructions for patterned tubular bands. Plates 25 and 26 show tubular band edgings on Bolivian textiles.

A backstrap setup is necessary to weave a tubular edge.

Thread the weft on a needle. Apply the tube to a selvage or to a seam.

Open a shed. Pass the weft from right to left and take a stitch into the fabric from the bottom up.

Change the shed. Tighten the weft and repeat the pass weft-stitch process.

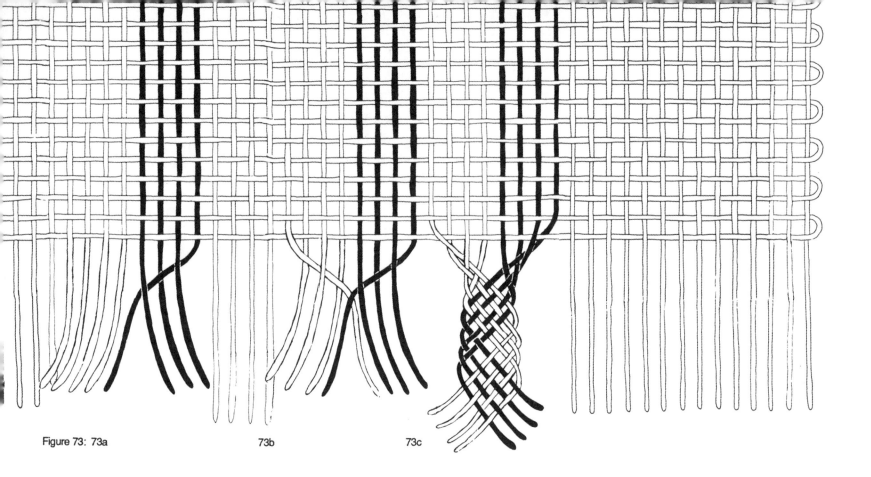

Figure 73: 73a   73b   73c

FINGER WEAVING

Finger Weaving is a flat braiding process that can be done when a strip with a bias quality is needed. (It could also be done on the warp ends of a piece as a fringe treatment.) There are many styles of fingerweaving. Consult the Turner book listed in the bibliography for the complete range. The Scandinavian style of braiding from the outside to the center is illustrated in figure 73.

Weave the outer right strand under and over the rest of the right-side warp ends until it reaches the center (fig. 73a). *Then repeat the weaving process with the outer left strand, crossing it under the right-center previously woven strand* (fig. 73b). Figure 73c shows the completed braid.

The bias nature of this type of band has "give" and can be used on curves or shaped pieces.

73d

44

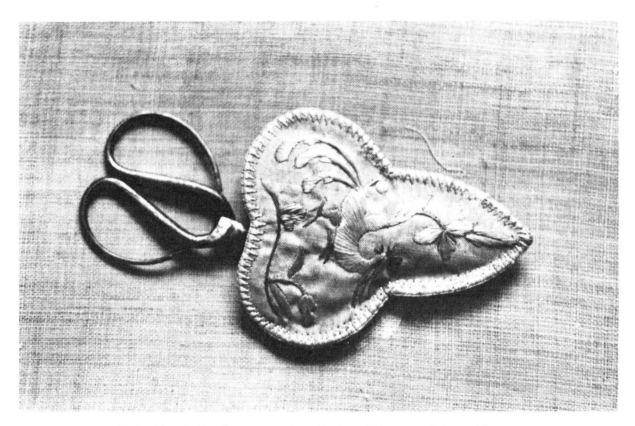

Embroidered silk scissors case from Northern China, actual size, with edging of Buttonhole Stitch variation. *Courtesy of Margaret McCutchan.*

Other Yarn Embellishments

There are a great many other yarn embellishments. The sennits and braids discussed in part II are very useful as trimmings. Inkle bands and card weaving are also excellent embellishments. Knitted bias strips and spool knitting are useful techniques for trims as well.

Remember that crochet and knitting combine well with weaving. Collars and cuffs on a garment may be knit or crocheted onto selvage and hemmed edges. Decorative edgings and trims may be knit or crocheted on as well. Lace enthusiasts may employ techniques of tatting and bobbin lace. Embroidery enthusiasts may use openwork embroidery techniques. There are endless possibilities.

Appendix I:

A Finishes & Embellishments Sampler

You may wish to make a notebook of samples to accompany the instructions in this book, in order to see how the various edges and trums look "in person." This will enable you to choose those techniques most relevant to the pieces to be finished, and to plan ahead for the necessary fringe allowances or seam allowances.

Figure 74

For a handy reference guide, our students punch holes along the edges of manilla folders and "apply fringe" to these holes with snitch knots. This provides a ready set of "warp ends" on which to try out the various knotted edgings and braids. See figure 74.

A piece of burlap with a few threads pulled out in the center, is a suitable edge on which to apply the stitched weft protectors. The various hemming stitches can be tried out on the sides of the burlap. Turn up the edges and stitch. See figure 75 a,c.

To practice the joining stitches, burlap may again be used. Draw lines on it with a marking pen to simulate seams. See figure 75b.

Various yarns can be used to try out the embellishments. Soft yarns such as knitting yarns are good for the tassels and pom-poms.

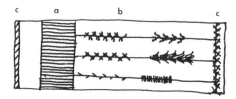

Figure 75

Fingering yarn is a good size for trying the Bolivian pom poms.

A stiff cord such as seine twine is excellent for the Monkey's Fist. Experiment with different sizes and textures of yarn in the braids and embellishments.

Appendix II:

Making a Butterfly

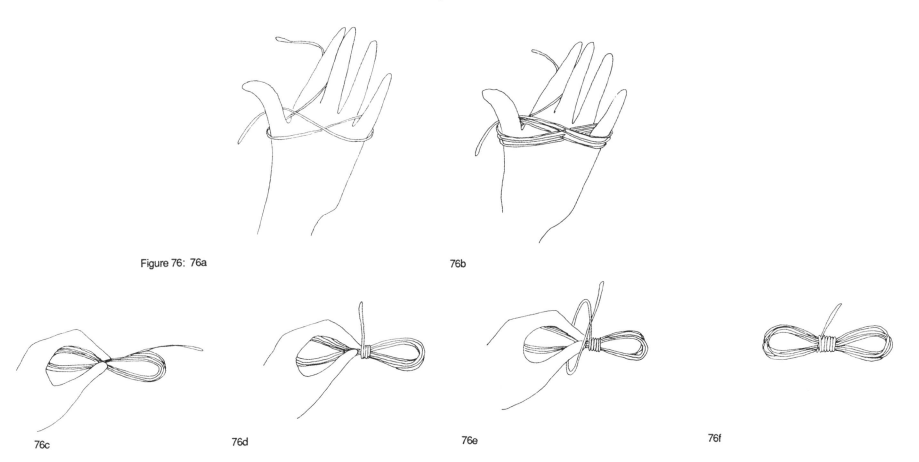

Figure 76: 76a   76b

76c   76d   76e   76f

When working knotting or braiding techniques with long strands of yarn, it may be helpful to wind each strand into a butterfly to shorten it. Figure 76 shows the winding process. Hold the end of the strand aside, as in figure 76a. Wind the yarn around the thumb and forefinger in a figure-eight (fig. 76b). Note: if you are working with a warp end, begin winding at the point nearest the cloth. Tie this figure-eight skein twice at the center with the winding end of the yarn (fig. 76d,e). The end that was held back will feed as needed (fig. 76f).

Bibliography

Atwater, Mary M., *Byways in Handweaving*, MacMillan, New York, 1954. (Unusual band weaving techniques.)

"   "   , *The Shuttlecraft Book of American Handweaving*, rev. ed., MacMillan, New York, 1956. (Has a good section on finishing.)

Baizerman, Suzanne, "Hemstitching for Linens," *The Weavers Journal*, Vol. 10, No. 3, Winter 1986.

"   "   , "Knotted Chinese Button," *The Weavers Journal*, Vol. 9, No. 1, Summer 1984.

Barker, June, *Decorative Braiding and Knotting*, Branford, Newton Center, Mass., 1973. (Great ideas for unusual braids.)

Black, Mary, *New Key to Weaving*, Bruce, New York, 1949. (Finishes on the loom and other good pointers.)

Brooks, Marguerite G., "Fringes from Warp Ends," *Handweaver and Craftsman*, Vol. 5, No. 1, Winter 1954.

Burchette, Dorothy, *Needlework Blocking and Finishing*, Scribner's, New York, 1974.

Cahlander and Cason, "A Tubular Edge Binding from Bolivia," *The Weavers Journal*, April 1977.

Cahlander, Adele, "Andean Crossed Warp Techniques for Decorative Trims, Parts I and II," *The Weavers Journal*, April 1978 and July 1978. (Flat and tubular band edgings.)

Cahlander, Adele, with M. Cason and A. Houston, "Bolivian Tubular Edgings and Crossed Warp Techniques," Monograph No. 1, *The Weavers Journal*, 1978. (A reprint of the above articles.)

Cahlander, Adele, *Sling Braiding of the Andes*, Colorado Fiber Center, Boulder, Colorado, 1980. (Interesting multi-strand braids .)

Cason and Cahlander, *The Art of Bolivian Highland Weaving*, Watson-Guptill, New York, 1976. (Great chapter on Bolivian finishing techniques.)

Collingwood, Peter, *The Techniques of Rug Weaving*, Watson-Guptill, New York, 1969. (The ultimate source on warp and weft protectors.)

Creys, Katharine, *Finishing and Mounting Your Needlepoint Pieces*, Crowell, 1973.

De Dillmont, Therese, *The Encyclopedia of Needlework*, Mulhouse, Alsace, France, 1880. Running Press, Philadelphia, 1972. (Great all-around reference; fancy hemstitching among many other things.)

D'Harcourt, Raoul, *Ancient Peruvian Textiles and their Techniques*, University of Washington Press, Seattle, 1962. (Inspirational--the Peruvians were master finishers!)

Ericson, Lois and Diane, *The Bag Book*, Van Nostrand Reinhold, New York, 1976. (Good purse finishes.)

Enthoven, Jacqueline, *The Stitches of Creative Embroidery*, Van Nostrand Reinhold, New York, 1964. (A reference for basic embroidery techniques.)

Gehret, Ellen J., *Rural Pennsylvania Clothing*, Liberty Cap Books, York Pa., 1976. (Some interesting joins and closings.)

Goodman, Frances Schaill, *The Embroidery of Mexico and Guatemala*, Scribner's, New York, 1976.

Gotthoffer, Esther, "Guatemalan Finishes," *Handweaver and Craftsman*, Vol. 5, No. 1, Winter 1971. (Guatemalan tassels and joins.)

Graumont, Raoul and John Hensel, *Encyclopedia of Knots and Fancy Rope Work*, Maritime Press, New York, 1939. (Source for interesting knots.)

Gulick, Evelyn, "Make Your Selvages Talk," *Handweaver and Craftsman*, Vol. 17, No. 2, Spring 1954. (Scallops and other edges.)

Harvey, Virginia, *Macrame, The Art of Creative Knotting*, Van Nostrand Reinhold, New York, 1967. (Basic macrame techniques.)

"   "   , "Tassels," *Threads in Action*, Vol. 1, No. 2, December 1969.

"   "   , "If Square Knot was the Only Knot," *Threads in Action*, Vol. 2, No. 1, Winter 1970.

"   "   , "Pattern with the Overhand Knot, Parts I and II," *Threads In Action*, Vol. 3, No. 1, Fall 1971.

"   "   , "Looping, Parts I-IV," *Threads In Action*, Vol. 4, No. 3-Vol. 5, No. 1, Spring 1973-Fall 1973.

"   "   , "An Edge Finish from Yugoslavia," *Threads In Action*, Vol. 4, No. 3, Spring, 1973.

Held, Shirley, Weaving, *A Handbook for Fiber Craftsmen*, Holt, Rinehart and Winston, New York, 1973. (A short chapter on finishing.)

King, Bucky and Susan Gilmurray, "Finishes and Embellishments for the Handweaver," *Shuttle, Spindle and Dyepot*, Vol. 3, No. 4, Fall, 1972. (Very good concise information).

Kroncke, Grete, *Mounting Handicraft*, Van Nostrand Reinhold, New York, 1967. (Good chapter on purses.)

Marsten, Ena, "The Five Finger Braid," *Threads In Action*, Vol. 3, No. 1, Fall 1971.

Meilach, Dona, *Macrame: Creative Design in Knotting*, Crown, New York, 1971. (Basic macrame techniques.)

Naumann, Rose and Raymond Hull, *The Off-Loom Weaving Book*, Scribner's, New York, 1973. (Has a good chapter on finishing.)

O'Neale, Lila M., *Textiles of Highland Guatemala*, Carnegie Institute, Washington, D.C., 1945. (Inspirational.)

Pancake, C., Baizerman, S., Searle, K., "Stitched Finishes in the Guatemalan Tradition," *Handwoven*, Vol. 2, No. 5, Nov. 1981.

Paque, Joan Michaels, *Design Principles and Fiber Techniques*, J. Paque, Milwaukee, 1973. (Structural approach to fiber techniques.)

Peterson and Svennas, *Handbook of Stitches*, Van Nostrand Reinhold, New York 1970. (Basic embroidery stitches.)

Searle, Karen, "Cardwoven Fringe," *The Weaver's Journal*, Vol 10, No. 2, Fall 1985. (Latvian trim.)

"   "   "Firfletting, Fringe Treatment from Norway," *The Weavers Journal*, Vol. 9, No. 4, Spring 1985.

Speiser, Noemi, *Manual of Braiding*, N. Speiser, Basel, Switzerland, 1983. (Many complex braids.)

Steedsman, Nell, *Patterns on a Plain Weave*, N. Steedsman, 1959. (Very good ideas on selvages, joinings, hems.)

Trotzig, Liv and Astrid Aselsen, *Weaving Bands*, Von Nostrand Reinhold, New York, 1974. (Good basic band weaving techniques.)

Turner, Alta, *Finger Weaving: Indian Braiding*, Sterling, New York, 1973. (Many types of finger woven bands.)

West, Virginia, *Finishing Touches for the Handweaver*, Branford, Newton Centre, Mass., 1967; Interweave Press, 1988. (Hemstitching, fringes, joins, handles.)

Wilson, Erica, *Erica Wilson's Embroidery Book*, Scribner's, New York, 1973. (Basic embroidery stitches.)

Wilson, Jean, *Weaving is Creative*, Van Nostrand Reinhold, New York, 1972. (Several good chapters on finishing.)

Wilson, Jean with Jan Burhen, *Weaving You Can Wear*, Van Nostrand Reinhold, New York, 1973. (Nice finishing touches for garments.)

See also: books on embroidery, costume, lace, macrame, weaving, crochet, knitting.

Index

INDEX TO PLATES

Afterword

We have presented a panorama of useful finishes and embellishments and we hope that this booklet provides you with a technique that is just right for your project. Yet we have only skimmed the surface. The books and articles listed in the bibliography have many more ideas in store for you.

We urge all fiber craftsmen to think in terms of finishes at the outset of a piece--to plan and execute a unified, integrated piece down to the last loving detail.